About the author

Tom Bottomore taught at the London School of Economics 1952–64, was Head of the Department of Political Science, Sociology and Anthropology at Simon Fraser University, Vancouver 1965–7, and Professor of Sociology at the University of Sussex 1968–85. He is now Professor Emeritus. He was President of the British Sociological Association 1969–71, and of the International Sociological Association 1974–8.

He is author of numerous books, including most recently *Theories of Modern Capitalism* (1985), *The Socialist Economy: Theory and Practice* (1990), *Classes in Modern Society* (2nd edn 1991), *Between Marginalism and Marxism: The Economic Sociology of J. A. Schumpeter* (1992), *Citizenship and Social Class* with T. H. Marshall (1992) and *Elites and Society* (2nd edn 1993). He has also edited *A Dictionary of Marxist Thought* (2nd edn 1991) and co-edited with William Outhwaite the *Blackwell Dictionary of Twentieth Century Social Thought* (1992). He is editor of the journal *Socialism of the Future* published by Pluto Press, and is a member of the management board of the Spanish edition of the journal *Socialismo del Futura* published by Fundación Sistema, Madrid.

Political Sociology

Second Edition

Tom Bottomore

Pluto **Press**

This edition first published 1993 by
Pluto Press, 345 Archway Road, London N6 5AA

First edition published 1979
Copyright © Tom Bottomore 1979, 1993

The right of Tom Bottomore to be identified as
author of this work has been asserted by him
in accordance with the Copyright, Design and
Patents Act of 1988

British Library Cataloguing in Publication Data
A catalogue record for this book is available
from the British Library
ISBN 0 7453 0651 9 hbk
ISBN 0 7453 0652 7 pbk X

Designed and produced for Pluto Press
by Chase Production Services, Chipping Norton

Typeset from author's disks
by Stanford Desktop Publishing Services, Milton Keynes
Printed in Great Britain by T. J. Press

Contents

Introduction

Political sociology is concerned with power in its social context. By 'power' is meant here the ability of an individual or a social group to pursue a course of action (to make and implement decisions, and more broadly to determine the agenda for decision making) if necessary against the interests, and even against the opposition, of other individuals and groups. This statement is not intended as a full and adequate definition of the concept of power, but only as a preliminary delineation of a field of enquiry. There are diverse conceptualizations of power,[1] which have their place within particular theories of politics, and in the course of this book some of the principal conceptual difficulties in the construction of such theories will be more fully explored. In addition to the questions that may be raised about the central notion of 'power', there are others concerning such cognate notions as 'authority', 'influence' and 'force' or 'violence', which will also need to be examined in the context of particular theoretical schemes.

It is evident that power, in the broad sense that I have indicated, is an element in most, if not all, social relationships – in the family, religious associations, universities, trade unions and so on – and it is important to keep in mind this wider view of the domain of political enquiry. Nevertheless, the principal object of political sociology has been, and should be, the phenomenon of power at the level of an inclusive society (whether that society be a tribe, a nation state, an empire or some other type); the relations between such societies; and the social movements, organizations and institutions which are directly involved in the determination of such power. For it is in this sphere that power appears in its purest, most distinctive form, and only from this vantage point can its manifestations in other spheres and in other forms be properly understood.

It is impossible, in my view, to establish any significant theoretical distinction between political sociology and political science. At most there appear to be differences arising either from traditional preoccupations or from a convenient division of labour; for example, the particular interest that political scientists have shown in what may be called the 'machinery of government' – the apparatus and processes of legislation, administration and legal regulation – considered to some extent in isolation from the social context and treated in a mainly descriptive manner. What might be argued, on the other hand, is that modern political science (that is, something indistinguishable from political sociology) owes its characteristic development since the eighteenth century to the establishment of a clear distinction between the 'political' and the 'social', the constitution of 'society' as an object of systematic enquiry, and the consequent reflection upon the relations between political and social life.[2]

This distinction was originally formulated in the contrast between 'civil society' and the 'state', and it was expounded in different ways in the works of the Encyclopedists and Saint-Simon, in the studies by Scottish philosophers and historians, notably in Adam Ferguson's *An Essay on the History of Civil Society*, and in Hegel's writings on the philosophy of right and of the state. Subsequently it found a classic expression in Marx's (1859, Preface) statement of the underlying principle of his social theory:

> I was led by my studies to the conclusion that legal relations as well as forms of state could neither be understood by themselves, nor explained by the so-called general progress of the human mind, but that they are rooted in the material conditions of life, which are summed up by Hegel after the fashion of the English and French writers of the 18th century under the name civil society, and that the anatomy of civil society is to be sought in political economy.

This new conception of politics developed along with the emergence of a new type of society, modern capitalism, in which the system of production acquired a force and independence much greater than it had attained in other societies. Hence the partial equation of 'civil society' with 'bourgeois society', the recognition of the fundamental importance of political economy as a 'political' science, and the formulation, as a central problem of the age, of the relation between the sphere of production, property and labour on one side, and organized political power – the state – on the other. These preoccupations, and the context in which they appeared, were clearly expressed by Hegel in the *Philosophy of Right*, when he argued that 'the creation of civil society is the achievement of the modern world', and defined civil society in terms of the economists' model of the free market, in which the association of its members 'is brought about by their needs, by the legal system – the means to security of person and property – and by external organization for attaining their particular and common interests'.[3] In Hegel's view civil society poses a number of problems for resolution by the state; above all, the problem of the interrelated growth of wealth and poverty, and the social polarization and conflict which this produces.

It is not difficult to see how important these conceptions were for the development of Marx's theory. Marx's transformation of Hegel's thought involves principally a rejection of the idea of the state as a higher universal in which the contradictions of civil society can be overcome, and an assertion of the dependence of the state precisely upon the contradiction, within the capitalist mode of production, between wealth and poverty, and hence upon the conflict between the two classes – bourgeoisie and proletariat – which embody these contradictory aspects of society. The state is thus conceived as a dependent element of a total social process in which the principal moving forces are those which arise from a particular mode of production.

But there is another style of political thought which treats the relation between civil society and the state in a different way, and contributes to a different version of political sociology. An early expression of this alternative view is to be found in Tocqueville's (1835–40) 'new science of politics [which] is needed for a new world', a science which was concerned with the development of democracy, and the formation of a 'modern' society (by contrast with the *ancien régime*) in France, England and the US. The distinctive nature of Tocqueville's conception can be roughly indicated by saying that in observing the two revolutionary currents of the eighteenth century – the democratic revolution and the industrial revolution – which were creating the 'new world' he, unlike Marx, paid more attention to the former and attributed to it a greater significance in the shaping of modern societies. For whatever the sources of the democratic movement might be, its consequences, he thought, were clear: its main tendency was to produce social equality, by abolishing hereditary distinctions of rank, and by making all occupations, rewards and honours accessible to every member of society. This tendency had, in his judgement, both desirable and undesirable aspects. A democratic government would be likely to devote its activities to the wellbeing of the greatest number, and could establish a liberal, moderate and orderly society. On the other hand, the pursuit of social equality, 'an insatiable passion' in democratic communities according to Tocqueville, may come into conflict with the liberty of individuals, and in this contest the former is likely to prevail, tending in the extreme case to 'equality in slavery'.

Tocqueville did not ignore the context of industrial capitalism in which the democratic movement existed, as may be seen especially in his analysis of the revolutions of 1848,[4] but he attributed to a democratic political regime, influenced by geography, laws and traditions – and for that reason following a different path of development in different societies (he was interested above all in a comparison between America and France) – an independent effectiveness in determining the general condition of social life. This idea of the autonomy of politics was elaborated by many later thinkers, in a more conscious opposition to Marxism, and came to constitute one of the major poles of political theory from the end of the nineteenth century. In one form it is a distinctive feature of Max Weber's political sociology, evident in his account of the concentration of the means of administration, which he regards as parallel to, and just as significant as, the concentration of the means of production; and more generally in his preoccupation with the role of the nation state and with the independent influence of various political tendencies – especially the socialist movement – upon national politics. As Robert Nisbet (1966, p. 292) observed, there is in Weber 'a temper of mind very close to Tocqueville', and notably a similar, but perhaps more pronounced, pessimism in his appraisal of the future of individual liberty in societies which are dominated, not so much by the passion for equality (although this plays a part), as by forces of rationalization.

The importance of independent political forces was asserted in another form, embodying a more direct confrontation with Marxism, in the theory of elites as it was formulated by Mosca, and more intransigently by Pareto. According to Mosca (1896, p. 50):

> Among the constant facts and tendencies that are to be found in all political organisms, one is so obvious that it is apparent to the most casual eye. In all societies – from societies that are very meagrely developed and have barely attained the dawnings of civilization, down to the most advanced and powerful societies – two classes of people appear – a class that rules and a class that is ruled. The first class, always the less numerous, performs all political functions, monopolizes power and enjoys the advantages that power brings, whereas the second, the more numerous class, is directed and controlled by the first, in a manner that is now more or less legal, now more or less arbitrary and violent.

Pareto (1915–19) developed a version of this theory in which the rule of elites was presented as a universal, unvarying and unalterable fact of social life, the existence of which depended upon psychological differences between individuals; but Mosca qualified his initial conception by recognizing that historical changes in the composition of the elite, and in the relation between rulers and ruled, could occur under the influence of various 'social forces' which represented the numerous different interests in society.[5]

Each of the two schemes of thought that I have outlined can be presented in an extreme form – as many critics have been concerned to show – to assert either a more or less total autonomy of politics, or its more or less complete dependence upon other social forces, particularly those which emerge within the economic sphere. Thus Karl Popper, in *The Open Society and its Enemies*, argued that the Marxist theory of society implies the 'impotence of all politics', since the political system of a particular society at any time, and its transformation, are alike determined by non-political forces; and this view has been reiterated, in a variety of ways, in subsequent writing. On the other side, elite theories have often been interpreted as asserting that there is a fundamental similarity between the political systems of all societies – unaffected by the diversity of economic and social circumstances – which results either from the universally occurring disparity between the positions of an organized minority and the unorganized majority, or from some general uniformity in human nature and the unequal distribution of talents.

For the most part, however, the ideas on both sides have been expounded with many qualifications, and the fundamental problem of the relation between the 'political' and the 'social' has come to be conceived in a more complex fashion, taking account of reciprocal influences and of historical variations. Even so, this relation remains a focal point of controversy, in which Marxist theory (notwithstanding its inner diversity and the reappraisals of the role of the state undertaken by some recent thinkers) is broadly opposed to those theories which are more exclusively concerned with the independent effects of political institutions – with party systems or types of government and administration – or which analyze political life in terms of national communities rather than social classes.

This is not the only major issue which has given rise to conflicting theoretical schemes. In the political sociology of the past few decades there has been a general opposition between those who are mainly preoccupied with the functioning of existing political institutions, conceived as one element in a social system which tends toward a state of equilibrium; and those who concentrate their attention mainly upon the forces which tend to produce instability and potentialities for change.

The first of these conceptions is intimately associated with the functionalist theory, which was especially influential in sociology during the 1950s and conveyed an image of society as an integrated system which is maintained in existence by complementary relationships between its various elements, or sub-systems, and rests ultimately upon a set of common values. It was in terms of this image or model that the notion of 'stable democracies' (which will be examined more closely in Chapter 1) was propounded, and the same general model shaped much of the discussion of 'development' and 'modernization', which were conceived largely as a process whereby agrarian societies gradually adapted to the conditions of life, values and institutions of the present-day industrial societies. Such a view was vigorously expounded, for instance, in Huntington's *Political Order in Changing Societies* (1968), which began from the proposition that 'the most important political distinction among countries concerns ... their degree of government', and then proceeded to distinguish between countries 'whose politics embodies consensus, community, legitimacy, organization, stability' and those which lack these qualities but display instead such features as intense ethnic and class conflict, rioting and mob violence, fragmentation of parties. In this manner, stability was enshrined as the highest political value, most fully exemplified in the politics of the democratic industrial societies.

Such ideas lost much of their persuasiveness after the resurgence of acute political conflict in the industrial societies during the 1960s, and subsequently, in the 1980s, the onset of conditions of economic and political crisis which still show no sign of reaching an end. As a consequence there was, in the first place, a marked renewal of interest in the alternative model, broadly Marxist in inspiration, which takes as its starting point the existence of strains, contradictions and conflicts in all social systems, and treats the maintenance of order and stability as only a partial and temporary (though in historical terms not necessarily short-lived) resolution of the various antagonisms. It is also a characteristic of this model that it assigns a larger place to the use of force, as against a general commitment to 'common values', in producing and reproducing a particular form of society; while values themselves, and the whole cultural system which they inform, may be regarded as being constituted largely by the exercise of 'symbolic violence',[6] not by some uncoerced process of intellectual agreement.

This is not to say, however, that in such a model, and more specifically in the Marxist theory, political domination has to be conceived as being based exclusively, or even mainly in most cases, upon the use of force; its effectiveness in assuring the continuance of an established social system arises from a complex set of conditions which may include economic domination, control over the reproduction of cultural values, and the superior organization of minorities. In short, the model proposes, in one of its versions at least, a conception of political domination as being grounded in a more general 'social power'. With the emergence of palpable strains and dissension in the Communist societies of Eastern Europe during the 1980s, culminating in the collapse of these regimes, the influence of Marxist thought, in so far as it was identified with an official and imposed state ideology, has receded. Nevertheless, the model emphasizing opposition and conflict in society to which Marxism made a major contribution is still influential, and can indeed be used fruitfully to analyze the changes that have occurred in Eastern Europe.

Taken together these two sets of opposed conceptions – autonomy versus dependence of political forces; stability, integration and determination by values versus mutability, contradiction and the use of force as pre-eminent characteristics of social systems – provide four possible models, to one or other of which the theories and investigations with which I shall be concerned in this book can be more or less adequately assimilated. But this still does not exhaust the diversity of conceptions prevalent in political sociology. The methodological disagreements among social scientists find expression also in political studies; and since commitment to a particular view or method has important consequences for the choice of problems, the conduct of enquiry and the mode of reasoning, it is desirable to examine here, however briefly, the principal issues involved, more particularly because they have often been presented in a narrow and over-simple way.

One major, long-standing disagreement separates those who think that there are no essential differences between the natural sciences and the social sciences and hence aim to provide a causal account of social events, from those who reject the idea of a social science in this sense and hold that the study of human society consists in understanding the meaning of intentional, rule-governed action by human agents.[7] The controversy has been carried on in several forms: in the criticism of 'positivism' from the standpoint of an 'interpretive' (*verstehende*) method, notably in the debate among German sociologists and historians which began in the latter part of the nineteenth century and has been resumed in a wider context in the past two decades; in the criticisms of the social sciences from a phenomenological or hermeneutic perspective; and on the other side the reassertion of the scientific character of the social sciences by those who espouse a structuralist or scientific realist view.[8] Over a

considerable period of time also, there have been major disputes among
Marxist thinkers between those who inclined towards a natural science
view – formulated in quite different ways by the Austro-Marxists at the
beginning of this century and by Althusser more recently – and those
who conceived Marxism rather as a philosophical interpretation of
history, in the manner of Lukács, Gramsci, the Frankfurt School and,
with various qualifications, such 'critical theorists' as Habermas.[9]
Although in political theory itself this methodological debate has not
been so extensively and systematically pursued as in sociology or in the
philosophy of science, much of the wider discussion impinges upon
problems in the study of politics, as for example in the work of
Poulantzas (1968) and others on the state and in Habermas' (1976)
discussion of legitimation. More specifically, the 'behavioural movement',
which was often considered to have brought about a radical reorientation of political science in the postwar period, tends no doubt towards
a natural science view, but without being committed to such a position;
for its general prescription that we should pay attention rather to actual
political behaviour than to the formal structure of institutions may be
followed in different ways according to whether 'behaviour' is conceived
as directly observable activity which can be causally explained, or as intentional action, the meaning of which has to be interpreted. In this sense
a phenomenological analysis of everyday political life would seem to be
just as acceptable as a strict behaviourist account along the lines suggested
in B. F. Skinner's *Beyond Freedom and Dignity*.

A second methodological debate, in which the principal contributions have come from recent Marxist and structuralist thinkers, concerns
empiricism. These thinkers, without by any means entering into all the
complexities of the problem,[10] have formulated various objections to
the empiricism – defined as the view that scientific knowledge is based
upon, and testable by, the observation and collection of 'given' facts –
which they believe prevails in the social sciences. They argue, first, that
a science does not develop by the collection of directly observable facts,
but by the elaboration of concepts which define the facts constituting
its domain; and second, that this theoretical activity involves the
discovery and analysis of a reality beyond what is immediately perceived.
As Godelier (1974) remarks, contrasting empiricist and structuralist
conceptions of social structure:

> For Marx as for Lévi-Strauss a structure is not a reality that is directly
> visible, and so directly observable, but a level of reality that exists
> beyond the visible relations between men, and the functioning of

which constitutes the underlying logic of the system, the subjacent
order by which the apparent order is to be explained.·[11]

Such ideas, which are by now quite familiar and widely accepted in
various philosophies of science, seem relevant, however, mainly to
naive forms of empiricism and inductivism, and they are not always
helpful in dealing with issues of verification or falsification, the assessment
of rival theories, or the demarcation of science from non-science.
Hence the various attempts, some of which are discussed in the volume
edited by Lakatos and Musgrave (1970), to formulate more sophisticated
versions of the notion of empirical testability.

Structuralism set itself in opposition not only to the cruder forms of
empiricism, as I have indicated, but also to historicism, thus renewing
the controversies about the historical method in the social sciences. The
question here does not concern the contrast between a 'generalizing'
and an 'individualizing' science (as Rickert expressed it) which belongs
rather to the debate about natural science and social science, but the
proper character of a generalizing science of society itself: whether its
aim should be to formulate universal statements about social structures
and their elements (for example, about the underlying structure of
kinship, of political relations and so on), or about cultural codes (by a
structural analysis of myth, for instance); or, on the contrary, to frame
historical laws, as was the ambition of the social evolutionists. These rival
views appear in a particularly interesting form in Marxist thought,
where the representation of Marxism as a philosophy of history, or a
'theory of the historical process' (Lukacs), was rejected by structuralist
thinkers, who conceived Marxism as a theory of society, 'a hypothesis
regarding the articulation of its internal levels and the specific hierarchical causality of each of these levels' [12], but who nevertheless still had
to confront the question posed by Marx's sketch of a definite sequence
of forms of society – as to whether there can be a science of history,
that is, a causal account of the transformation of one structure into
another in some law-governed and necessary process.

This opposition raises the last of the methodological issues that I intend
to consider here: namely, whether there is in fact, as has quite frequently
been claimed, a distinctive Marxist method, and if so, how it is to be
characterized. The preceding discussion may already suggest a negative
answer. There is not just one version of Marxism, but several; and each
version – elements of which are certainly to be found in Marx's own
work – presents a view of method which agrees in some measure with
the ideas of non-Marxist thinkers and is influenced by general movements

of thought in the philosophy of science. In broad terms, it is possible to distinguish at least three main styles of Marxist social theory: the Hegelian, which has affinities with the 'interpretive' method and with a phenomenological approach; the positivist–empiricist, and more recently the scientific realist, influenced in various ways by neo-Kantian epistemology, by natural science models, and by materialism; and the structuralist, which has its principal sources in structural linguistics and anthropology, and in French epistemological doctrines (especially the work of Bachelard), though it also has affinities with scientific realism.

Faced with this diversity of methods it may be claimed instead that what is distinctive about Marxism is a central core of theoretical concepts and propositions; but this does not fully resolve the difficulty, for theory and method are interconnected, and the divergent Marxist conceptions express both conceptual and methodological disagreements. It is more instructive perhaps to think of the different versions of Marxism as competing paradigms,[13] and then to ask whether the family resemblances among them are nevertheless so great that at a more general level they can reasonably be contrasted as a whole with other paradigms that are distinctly non-Marxist. In my view this is largely the case, although it has to be recognized that there are other family resemblances which cut across this particular division, and that the boundary between Marxist and non-Marxist social theory is in any case neither clearly nor permanently marked. Marxism is not a closed scheme of thought impervious to outside influences, and it may happen, for example, that a phenomenological Marxist has closer intellectual affinities with other phenomenologists than with other Marxists.

In so far as Marxism can be distinguished more or less clearly, as a general paradigm, from other paradigms, it also raises in a particularly striking form two issues which are not primarily theoretical or methodological; one concerning the general relation of political sociology to practical social life, the other the diverse ideological orientations it may assume. As to the first, the difference between Marxism and other social thought is not that in one case the connection between theory and practice is consciously acknowledged and asserted, while in the other it is not – for this connection appears in all social thought, although with varying degrees of clarity – but that practice is conceived, in Marx's phrase, as 'revolutionary, practical-critical activity'. As Lukács (1923) subsequently argued, Marxist theory 'is essentially nothing more than the expression in thought of the revolutionary process itself'. This view of theory and practice conveys, if only implicitly, a definite ideology. A Marxist social scientist is not only intellectually persuaded of the theoretical and methodological superiority of Marxism, but also espouses – however varied and imprecise the manner of doing so – a more general world view in which such ideas as 'revolution', 'classless society', the 'end of alienation', 'socialism' or a new 'integral civilization' (for which, according to Gramsci, Marxism provides the fundamental elements) express value judgements on existing forms of society, affirm beliefs in the possibility and desirability of a new kind of society and hence stimulate and guide distinctive kinds of political activity.

In a similar way, though not always so obviously, other social theories or paradigms express other values and beliefs, direct both theory and practice into other channels, through their conceptions of 'democracy', 'nation' or 'liberal society', and may likewise become predominantly ideological. These crucial questions of the relation between political sociology and political action arise inescapably throughout this book and will be more closely examined in Chapter 6.

The multiplicity of paradigms (briefly indicated in the preceding discussion) which characterizes the social sciences today excludes any possibility of setting out in a direct and uncontroversial way the 'elements' or 'principles' of political sociology. What the subject is, the problems and solutions which constitute it as a field of scientific enquiry, its development through the accumulation of knowledge and techniques, or through scientific revolutions, can only be established by confronting the different paradigms with each other and seeing them in the context of a historical process that embraces not only the progress of the science itself, borne along by diverse groups of thinkers and researchers, but also the unceasing transformation of its external environment as a result of economic, political and cultural changes. Thus in the following chapters I shall present competing paradigms and consider them in their social and cultural settings; and I shall ask what distinctive, alternative or incommensurable views of the political world, what judgements about its fundamental elements and their interrelations, about the crucial questions that should be posed and the methods of investigation that should be used, divide the various groups of researchers and schools of thought.

1 Democracy and Social Classes

The pre-eminent themes of political sociology in its formative period during the first half of the nineteenth century were the social consequences of the emergence of democracy as a form of government and the political significance of the development of social classes on the basis of industrial capitalism. To some extent, as I have suggested in the Introduction, these two themes were conceived in ways which gave rise to antithetical theories, in which either the influence of political forms and forces upon society or the influence of various social elements upon political forms was more strongly emphasized. This opposition in the realm of ideas corresponds partly, it may be argued, to an antithesis in social reality, between the human being as a citizen – as a member of a community endowed with equal civil and political rights – and as a member of civil society – an egoistic individual whose situation is determined by private interests within the economic system.[1] In whatever fashion the contrast is formulated (we might say, for example, that the two revolutions – political and industrial – which had inspired the new political science began to move in different directions, towards greater equality in one case, away from it in the other) it embodies a large part of the substance of political enquiry and of political doctrines from the nineteenth century to the present time.

Hence a theory of democracy and a theory of social classes are essential elements in the construction of a science of politics and an examination of the development of these theories will help to clarify its nature and problems. We can take as one starting point Tocqueville's conception of democracy, which I have already briefly sketched in the Introduction. It has often been pointed out by commentators that there is an ambiguity in Tocqueville's discussion. At times he is chiefly concerned with democracy as a form of government, when he describes it as a regime in which 'the people more or less participate in their government', and says that 'its meaning is intimately connected with the idea of political liberty'; while on other occasions he uses the term 'democracy' to describe a type of society, and refers more broadly to 'democratic institutions' and by implication to what would later be called a 'democratic way of life'.[2] Nevertheless, it is fairly clear that he saw the democratic political movement as the principal force creating this new social order; for it is the democratic regime that assigns pre-eminent value to the wellbeing of the greatest number, establishes an open and mobile society by destroying the old hierarchy of ranks, and encourages the development of trade and manufacture. Of course, Tocqueville recognized that the development of the industrial system itself might have important effects upon the democratic regime, especially through the emergence in productive industry of a new 'aristocracy', but he was inclined to regard this as an exceptional and temporary phenomenon which would not be able to withstand the general tendency of democracy to bring about greater equality.

The theory of social classes, first comprehensively formulated by Marx, approaches the same problem from the other side by seeking to explain democracy as the consequence of changes in society. According to this view the democratic political revolutions were carried out by a new class – the bourgeoisie – which was formed in the process of development of commercial and industrial capitalism; and the future of democracy would be vitally affected by the inherent tendencies of capitalist production and the relation between the bourgeoisie and the other new class in capitalist society – the proletariat. The crucial political issue for Marx, and for those who were subsequently influenced by his theory, was the 'social question'; that is, the situation, interests and struggles of the working class in societies which were both capitalist and democratic. Hence the question of democracy is placed in a broader social context, in which a predominant element is the interests and political orientations of social classes which are in conflict with each other. This does not mean that democracy is conceived only as the political form assumed by the rule of the bourgeoisie, even though it is historically an achievement of the bourgeoisie, a real advance upon the preceding forms of government and a 'progressive' feature of capitalism. Marx sees, rather, a tension or contradiction between the principle of democracy – the full participation of all members of society in regulating their communal life – and the limited, even distorted form which democracy assumes in a class society in which the bourgeoisie is dominant. For Marx, democracy is a historical phenomenon which is far from having unfolded all its possibilities, and the principal agent of its further development is the working-class movement.

Although Tocqueville and Marx emphasized different features in the development of European and North American societies in the

nineteenth century, they both recognized in some way the interplay of
economic and political forces: Tocqueville by associating democracy with
the values of an agricultural and commercial middle-class society, and
by noting the possible implications of the incipient class divisions
within manufacturing industry; Marx by giving prominence to the
political struggles of the working class as a movement to extend
democracy, whether in his account (in 1852) of the Chartist demand
for universal suffrage as being, if realized, 'a far more socialist measure
than anything which has been honoured with that name on the
Continent', or in his later analysis of the Paris Commune (1871) as a
new form of democratic government, as 'the political form at last
discovered under which to work out the emancipation of labour'.
This developing interaction between democracy, capitalism and social
classes, further complicated by nationalism, constitutes the political
history of the past century, and is the subject matter of the most
important political theories of this period.

We should note, in the first place, how very slow the advance of
democracy has been, and how many hindrances and setbacks it has
encountered. In those countries which have generally been regarded as
well-established democracies, manhood suffrage was only achieved in
most cases between the end of the nineteenth century and the First World
War, while the attainment of universal and equal suffrage came still later
(in Germany in 1919, Sweden in 1920, France in 1945, Britain in 1948)[3]
while in most of the rest of the world universal suffrage, where it was
introduced at all, came only after the end of the Second World War.
There are still countries – South Africa being one example – where the
great majority of people have never had more than a very restricted right
to vote, and many others in which this right has, at various times, been
curtailed or abrogated. In Europe between the wars fascist movements
destroyed democracy in several countries, while in Latin America,
Africa and Asia military dictatorships and other forms of authoritarian
rule have been common, and continue to exist in many places. In the
former regimes of 'real socialism' in Eastern Europe the right to vote
was largely denuded of its meaning by the proscription of any opposition
parties, and even of dissenting groups within or outside the single
ruling party, while the movements for democratic reform which
emerged in the 1950s and 1960s were regularly suppressed by force or
intimidation until they were finally successful at the end of the 1980s.

It can scarcely be claimed, therefore, that the political systems of the
world in the mid-twentieth century revealed a very widespread practice
of democracy – though the principle was more widely asserted – even

in the narrow constitutional sense of the right of all adult citizens to choose their political leaders by means of free elections. Democracy has been a very recent, delicate and somewhat sparse growth, continually threatened and often stifled by property-owning, privileged and dominant groups who are always fearful of any autonomous, unregulated incursion of the 'masses' into politics. This will become more evident if we go on to consider democracy in its larger sense as a state of affairs in which all citizens participate, and are encouraged to participate, as fully as possible in the organization and regulation of their whole social life. Here we need to pay attention to two aspects: first, the obstacles which have been placed, and are continually placed, in the way of such participation in practice; and second, the reinterpretations of democracy, within political sociology as well as in political doctrines, which seek deliberately to restrict its scope.

The evidence of these obstacles and resistances is plain enough, not only in the slow, uncertain and frequently subverted extension of the right to vote which I have already indicated, but in the bitter hostility and violence that has always been directed against the attempts of ordinary citizens and workers to organize themselves in trade unions, cooperatives, community action groups, and similar bodies. The early history of the trade union movement, in particular, is one of intimidation and repression by ruling groups ranging from imprisonment and deportation to the use of hired gunmen and military forces in attempts to prevent the formation of trade unions or to break strikes; and in some countries – notably in the US[4] – the use of violence, though usually diminishing, has continued until recent times. Other popular movements of protest and reform have often been met by violence – for example, the civil rights movement of the 1960s in the US, and on a larger scale the diverse movements in Eastern Europe, as well as in many parts of the Third World, which have been suppressed by military force.

But the use of violence to restrict democracy, though it is still very prevalent in some regions of the world, is far from being the only means by which such limitations are imposed. There is, even in those societies which have established democratic institutions in the form of competing parties, free elections and a more or less independent (though not necessarily impartial) judiciary, a persistent discouragement of any political action which takes place outside the traditional framework of party politics and electoral contests. One example can be found in the response of ruling groups and elites to the student movement of the 1960s. Even if we disregard the sporadic use of violence against the movement, and its infiltration by spies and *agents provocateurs*, it is clear that it was generally considered by the controlling bodies of universities and by party politicians as an illegitimate form of political action, even though its principal aim was to extend democratic participation in one of the most important institutions (both economically and culturally) of modern society, and in many cases it succeeded in enlivening academic studies, as well as improving methods of teaching and assessment. Movements for industrial democracy have been similarly discouraged, and even socialist governments, whether reformist or revolutionary, have shown little enthusiasm for a devolution of their powers which would permit a greater involvement of ordinary people in the direction of their everyday economic activities. On the contrary, with the exception of Yugoslavia, where the system of workers' self-management did something to diffuse responsibility for decision making, there has been a tendency towards increasingly centralized and bureaucratic administration in economic and other spheres of social life.[5]

The antipathy to any large-scale popular participation in running public affairs, which shows itself constantly in many more forms than those which I have mentioned here by way of illustration, has been incorporated in several different ways into political science. Leaving aside here the more extreme version of the theory of elites as expounded by Pareto or by Ortega y Gasset (1930, p. 49) in his distinction between the inert masses and 'the select men, the nobles, the only ones who are active and not merely reactive', we can identify two types of political theory which, while accepting some aspects of modern democracy, are concerned to limit its significance.

In the first case, democracy is conceived only as a means for selecting political leaders, and not as a regime in which there is some kind of direct rule by the people. This conception was formulated by Max Weber, in *Economy and Society* (1921), though in a rather fragmentary manner, and was expressed also in his criticism of German politics in *Parliament and Government in a Reconstructed Germany* (1919). According to Weber direct democracy is possible only in small and relatively simple societies, whereas beyond this stage, in societies which have become larger, more complex and more differentiated – and especially in modern societies – direct rule by the people is out of the question. It is replaced by representative democracy, and this means, in Weber's view, that the people cease to have any real control over political decisions, which become the prerogative, on one side, of a bureaucratic administration and, on the other side, of the leaders of political parties. Weber gives as reasons for this power position of the bureaucratic and political elites their possession of the means of administration and the fact that they are small groups which can easily reach agreement upon any action necessary to maintain their power.[6] In any case, Weber is not very much concerned about the absence of popular control over the political elites. For him the value of representative democracy resides in the fact that it makes possible the selection of effective political leaders,[7] as well as providing a training for them. In the circumstances prevailing in industrial societies, with their mass parties, the only viable kind of democracy is what he called a 'plebiscitarian leader-democracy', in which charismatic leaders set goals 'which are then to be "sold" to the people at large by "party machines", and afterwards implemented with the help of administrative bureaucracies'.[8]

Weber's argument was presented more systematically and in a somewhat different form, though with the same object in view, by Schumpeter (1942, chap. 21) who explicitly rejected the 'classical doctrine' of democracy, according to which it embodies distinctive ideals concerning participation in political life and the relationship between political leaders and the people, and replaced it by another theory of democracy as 'competition for political leadership': 'the democratic method is that institutional arrangement for arriving at political decisions in which individuals acquire the power to decide by means of a competitive struggle for the people's vote' (p. 269). The basis of his theory of democracy is a theory of capitalist enterprise, and Schumpeter emphasizes the connection not only by discussing the historical relation between capitalism and democracy, but by treating political parties as analogous to business concerns engaged in a competitive struggle (for power in one case, profits in the other) the aim of which for each party/enterprise is to increase its share of the market (constituted by voters or consumers). This conception, in the form of an 'economic theory of democracy', was further developed by later writers, and notably by Downs (1957) in whose scheme of analysis there are 'basically, only two kinds of actor. There are the parties, and there are the voters.'[9]

This restrictive conception of democracy as a technique for the selection of political leaders was one important influence leading political sociologists to devote their attention too exclusively to elections and voting behaviour. Indeed, this became for a time a veritable obsession, giving rise in some academic circles to the idea of a whole new field of study, to be called 'psephology',[10] and in the lower reaches of political communication to the massive television coverage of national elections, in which precise calculations of 'swings' from one party to another and predictions of the eventual outcome of the electoral contest tended to overshadow any serious discussion of the substance of political conflicts.

It is a further consequence of this conception that democracy comes to be seen as a more or less perfected instrument which is susceptible to only minor technical improvements; and in this respect there is agreement with a second notion of democracy, elaborated mainly during the postwar decades, which was expressed by the term 'stable democracy'. According to this view the existence of stable or viable democracy in a particular society depends primarily upon certain values being held by the people in that society; that is to say, upon the existence of an underlying consensus, or, as it was sometimes called, a common value system. Without entering upon a detailed examination of this idea,[11] let me simply observe, in the present context, that it too takes for granted that democracy, in the instances considered, has reached a stage of more or less completed development, and can thus be contrasted, as a distinct type of political system, with other types such as totalitarianism, dictatorship or 'unstable' democracy.

What Schumpeter called the 'classical doctrine' of democracy differs in several respects from the theories I have just outlined, one of the crucial differences being that it conceives democracy as a historical movement which aims constantly to extend the area within which the members of a society can govern themselves by participating fully and freely in the regulation of their collective life. To a great extent this democratic movement has to be seen as a class movement: first of the bourgeoisie seeking freedom from feudal constraints and aristocratic rule, and subsequently of the working class seeking its liberation from the domination of the bourgeoisie. Thus two stages of the movement can be distinguished: a stage of liberal democracy when a competitive political system was introduced alongside the market economy, and a stage of social democracy in which there is expressed the idea of the political dominance of the most numerous class – the working class – and of the transformation of the market economy into a socialist economy.

From this perspective the nature of modern democratic regimes, and the setbacks and limitations which they experience, are intimately connected with the class structure and the relations between classes as they have developed both in capitalist and in what I shall call (for the moment) post-capitalist societies. Marx's social theory, although it did not advance in any detail beyond the analysis of capitalism as a mode of production to a study of the state and politics, did none the less sketch a conception of political development which was assimilated into the doctrines and practices of a large part of the European labour movement.

The main elements of this conception can be set out very briefly in the following way.[12] With the development of the capitalist mode of production there is an intensification of two principal contradictions within capitalism; that between the forces of production and the social relations of production, and that between the working class and the bourgeoisie. The former contradiction, which Marx describes as 'the fundamental contradiction of developed capitalism', is one between the social character of production, with its tendency towards unlimited development of the productive forces, and the private ownership of the means of production (and therefore private appropriation of the product) from which derives the aim of maintaining and increasing the value of capital itself, and hence setting limits to the expansion of production.[13] The contradiction shows itself in the phenomena of underconsumption and in periodic crises; and it provides the main ground for Marx's expectation of an eventual breakdown of the capitalist system. Nevertheless, the breakdown is not seen by Marx as a fully determined and automatic consequence of capitalist economic development; on the contrary, as Nicolaus (1972, p. 328) has observed, Marx's theory of the breakdown is characterized by 'its great latitude and flexibility'.

It is at this point that the second contradiction – between working class and bourgeoisie – which differs from the first in expressing an opposition of interests rather than an incompatibility of structures, assumes great importance. The demise of capitalism can only be the consequence of a political struggle and it is the course of this struggle between classes, in the conditions created by the development of the capitalist mode of production, which we now have to examine. Marx's own theory of the class struggle was hardly more than sketched, in occasional passages which are scattered throughout his writings, and it was never presented in a systematic way. Moreover, the material upon which he had to work was that of the early stages of industrial capitalism and of the working-class political movement, so that in any case it would be essential to review his theory in the light of subsequent historical experience. This task, in any comprehensive sense, is beyond the scope of the present book, and I shall confine myself to a very schematic presentation of a few salient issues.

There are two broad sets of problems to be considered: first, the political impact of the working-class movement in capitalist societies as they have developed since the late nineteenth century; and second, the political systems that emerged from revolutions carried out under the banner of Marxism as 'proletarian revolutions', in Russia, China and other countries. As to the first question, it is evident that the working-class movement has had a profound influence upon the extension of the suffrage and the creation of mass parties (which will be examined further in Chapter 2), and hence upon the establishment of a democratic political regime as it now exists in the advanced capitalist countries. Furthermore, the pressure of working-class parties and trade unions has helped to produce a much more substantial intervention by the state in the economy, and this situation, although it can be interpreted from one aspect as the emergence of a new type of 'organized' or 'managed' capitalism, does also constitute a degree of protection of working-class interests against the power of capital through the general regulation of economic activity and the provision of an extensive network of social services, however imperfectly this may be done. But it is equally obvious that the working class in the advanced capitalist societies has not been, for the most part, revolutionary in its outlook and action; least of all in the US. It is not that revolutionary movements have been absent (and they will be considered in more detail in Chapter 4) but that they have failed to elicit sustained and effective support from any large part of the working class. Of course, there have been historical fluctuations in revolutionary activity, as well as considerable variations between societies – with revolutionary parties having had a greater influence in France and Italy than in the rest of Western and Northern Europe or in North America – but the predominant style of working-class politics everywhere has been reformist, directed toward a gradual attrition of the unregulated market economy. There has not occurred that stark polarization and revolutionary confrontation of the two principal classes – bourgeoisie and proletariat – that Marx, at least in some parts of his analysis, seemed to anticipate.

How is this historical development to be explained? In the first place, perhaps, as many social thinkers from Bernstein to Schumpeter and beyond have suggested, by the economic successes of capitalism. Although there have been periods of economic stagnation or crisis, including the exceptionally severe crisis of the 1930s (which itself failed to engender large-scale revolutionary movements in most of the capitalist countries), and a renewed depression in the 1980s, the general tendency of capitalism has been to promote a continuous, and sometimes rapid, improvement in material standards of living, in which a large part of the working class, if not the whole class, has shared. This factor of material prosperity, which was already cited by Sombart (1906) at the beginning of this century as a partial explanation of the absence of any large-scale socialist movement in the US, acquired particularly great importance in the period following the Second World War, when economic growth took place more rapidly than ever before, and the question could be posed as to whether the US did not simply show to capitalist Europe the image of its own future – a future that would be characterized by a decline of the socialist movement, and indeed of all ideological revolutionary parties and movements.[14]

This increasing prosperity is not, however, the only factor that can be adduced to explain the absence of successful revolutionary movements, or of such movements altogether, in Western capitalist societies. The class struggle, it may be argued, has been moderated by the incorporation of the working class into a modified and reformed capitalism through the extension of political, social and economic rights, and the elaboration of a complex structure of contestation, bargaining and compromise within the existing form of society. The class struggle is further moderated, and turned increasingly into reformist channels, by changes in the nature of the class structure, and notably by the growth of the middle classes.

Working-class action in the economic sphere, through the trade unions, necessarily takes place in the context of a factual interdependence between employers and workers, and this interdependence is reinforced by the institutionalization of industrial conflict. Durkheim (1893), in his discussion of the 'abnormal forms' of the division of labour, long ago drew attention to what he regarded as a condition of 'anomie' in the sphere of production, characterized by the absence of a body of rules governing the relations between different social functions – above all between labour and capital – and saw as both probable and desirable a growing normative regulation of industrial relations. This has in fact occurred in the advanced capitalist countries, and one main consequence has been to limit industrial conflict primarily to economic issues, as against larger issues of the control of the enterprise, and to bring about a substantial degree of integration of workers into the existing mode of production.[15] Hence it might be argued, as Marcuse (1964) and others did, that a large part of the Western working class has been effectively incorporated into the economy and society of advanced capitalism, not only in the sphere of consumption, as a result of increasing prosperity, but also in the sphere of production, through the increasingly elaborate regulation of industrial relations by law and custom, and through the apparent technological imperatives of a high productivity, high consumption society. The outcome may thus be seen as a situation in which there is considerable trade-union militancy with respect to wages, hours of work and related issues, but relatively little expression of class consciousness in the broader sense of any profound awareness or conviction of living in a society the nature of which is predominantly determined by class relations, and of being engaged in a continuing struggle to establish an alternative form of society.

There can be little doubt either that the development of working-class consciousness has been profoundly affected by changes in the class structure. The emergence and growth of new middle-class strata in the Western capitalist societies is a phenomenon which has raised questions for both Marxist and non-Marxist social scientists since the end of the nineteenth century. It was one important consideration in Bernstein's 'revision' of Marxist theory,[16] and the problem was later analyzed more fully by the Austro-Marxist thinkers, who came to recognize the political significance of the growing complexity of the class structure,[17] and in particular the influence of what Karl Renner called the 'service class'.[18] Among non-Marxist writers, especially during the 1950s, the expansion of these middle strata was often interpreted as marking the advent of middle-class societies in which there would be no fundamental cleavages or conflicts.[19] It is clear in any case that the growing size of the middle class must change fundamentally the image of capitalist society as one in which class antagonisms are simplified, and 'society as a whole is more and more splitting up into two great hostile camps, into two great classes directly facing each other – bourgeoisie and proletariat', which Marx and Engels depicted in the *Communist Manifesto* and which Marxists and other socialists generally accepted without much questioning until the early years of the twentieth century. The need then arises to analyze and evaluate the probable political attitudes and actions of various middle-class groups in relation to the working class and the socialist movement, to right-wing parties and movements, to fascist movements and to diverse types of independent politics in the form of liberal, nationalist or populist parties. Several different answers have been given to the questions thus raised. One, already mentioned, envisages a gradual consolidation of a new kind of middle-class, post-industrial society (Bell, 1973), based upon advanced technology, a mixed economy and a broad consensus of opinion about social and political goals, which would be peaceful, liberal and in a certain sense 'classless'.[20] Another foresees a more conservative role for the middle class, expressing itself in active opposition to socialism as a process of increasing public ownership or control of industry and expanding welfare services, and in a reassertion of the desirability of a more *laissez-faire* type of economy.[21]

A third kind of analysis conceives some sections of the middle class (technicians, managers, engineers, professional employees in the public service and in private industry) either as constituting an important part of a 'new working class' which is likely to participate in its own way in a refashioned socialist movement (Mallet, 1975), or as forming one element – alongside the old industrial working class – in a new class, which is becoming involved in a new type of struggle, directed against those who control the institutions of economic and political decision making, and who reduce it to a condition, not of misery or oppression, but of restricted and dependent participation in the major public affairs of society (Touraine, 1971a).[22]

One common theme in these varied accounts of the changing economy and class structure of the advanced capitalist societies is a questioning of the pre-eminent role of the industrial working class in bringing about a fundamental transformation of society from capitalism to socialism. But there has also been a wider questioning of the whole conception of a transition to socialism. What Schumpeter (1942) called the 'march into socialism' seems to have slackened its pace; and socialism, which appeared in the nineteenth century as the ideal image of an alternative society, providing an indispensable unifying element in working-class consciousness, has become in the late twentieth century a more problematic reality (Stojanović, 1973; Kolakowski and Hampshire, 1974; Parekh, 1975). It is not simply that the former communist societies in Eastern Europe were characterized, to a greater or lesser extent, by relative economic backwardness and political authoritarianism, and consequently had little appeal as models for the future development of any advanced industrial society, but that the democratic socialism of social democratic and labour parties in the capitalist world, despite its real achievements in improving the conditions of life of the working class, has come to be more critically judged as tending to promote an excessive centralization of decision making, growth of bureaucracy and regulation of the lives of individuals, and has lost something of the persuasive character it once had as a movement aiming to create a new civilization. Such changes in social and political thought clearly have important consequences for the character and goals of political action in the late twentieth century, and their effects are reinforced by the emergence of new problems and new movements – concerned with such issues as the environment and the use of natural resources, and the subordination of women – which arguably have little connection with class politics; as well as by the renewed vigour of ethnic and national consciousness, expressed in independence movements of various kinds.

To speak of these 'new styles' of politics is not, of course, to say that political struggles between classes have ceased, but only that they may now be modified by other kinds of political action and be less predominant in political life as a whole; or to argue that the nature, aims and strategies of the principal classes have changed substantially, as Mallet and Touraine have suggested. Undoubtedly, the two interrelated movements — the democratic movement and the labour movement — which developed so vigorously in the nineteenth century continue to have a major influence in politics, but the relation between them has changed during the present century, in a way which is also relevant to the character of more recent movements. In large measure, the nineteenth-century labour movement could be regarded — and regarded itself — as a continuation of the democratic movement, this continuity being expressed even in the name 'social democratic' which was widely adopted by the political parties of the working class. The idea which lay behind the use of the term 'social democracy' was that the working-class movement would not only complete the process of achieving political democracy by establishing universal and equal suffrage (and this itself required a long struggle), but would also extend democracy into other areas of social life, in particular through a democratic control of the economy, and would thus create new democratic institutions. One of the most important of these institutions was the workers' council, which made its appearance in the early part of this century as a method of establishing direct working-class control of production, in opposition to both capitalist ownership and centralized state control. The 'council movement' was especially vigorous, and was widely debated among socialists in the years immediately preceding and following the First World War (Renner, 1921; Pribicevic, 1959); and more recently it again aroused growing interest as a result of the experience of workers' self-management in Yugoslavia, some tentative steps in that direction in other East European countries during the 1970s, and the formulation of ideas about 'participatory democracy' that arose from the new social movements of the late 1960s.[23]

While they advocated and worked for such extensions of democracy the European social democratic parties, whether or not they claimed to be Marxist and revolutionary, were also, for the most part, firmly committed to political democracy in the narrower sense; and where the necessary conditions were present — the legal existence of socialist parties, elections conducted on the basis of (at least) universal male suffrage, and participation in parliament and government — they made plain that although they did not renounce extra-parliamentary forms of class action they envisaged the transition from capitalism to socialism as coming about through the will of a majority of citizens, clearly and publicly expressed in elections. These issues were perhaps most thoroughly discussed, and the idea of a peaceful and democratic conquest of power by the working class most adequately expressed, by the Austrian Social Democratic Party, at its annual conferences and in the writings of its leading thinkers.[24] But the Russian Revolution of 1917 and the subsequent development of Soviet society produced an emphasis upon another strand in Marxist thought about the transition to socialism (one which had not hitherto been given much prominence) involving the idea of the 'dictatorship of the proletariat'; and in the specific conditions prevailing in Russia, which differed entirely from those in Western Europe, this soon evolved in practice into the dictatorship of the Bolshevik party, then the dictatorship of the party's central committee, and finally the dictatorship of a single individual. For several decades, therefore, one important section of the working-class movement and one school of socialist thought became identified with an authoritarian – and for more than twenty years tyrannical – form of government. Only after the death of Stalin, with the emergence of movements of opposition, and rebellions, in the Soviet sphere of influence did this situation begin to change; and the eventual collapse of these regimes has now eliminated that version of socialism from the political map of Europe.

During the postwar period the idea of democracy also came to be expressed in new terms – differing profoundly from the restrictive meaning which Schumpeter, Weber and others had imparted to it – through its association with the idea of citizenship. The classic statement of this view by T. H. Marshall (1950; reprinted in Marshall and Bottomore, 1992) conceived citizenship as a condition in which all members of a society possessed clearly defined and steadily expanding civil, political and social rights; and in this sense it embodied a principle of equality which brought it into conflict with the inequalities engendered by a capitalist economy or existing in various authoritarian regimes. There was implicit in it, therefore, in the case of Western societies, the idea of a movement towards socialism, particularly when the development of social rights was more strongly emphasized by the creation of welfare states.

Citizenship, regarded in this way, has played an increasingly important part in political thought and controversy during the past few decades. First, in the communist societies, the assertion of basic civil and political rights was a major element in the programmes of the opposition movements, and such ideas were also widely diffused in the 1970s and 1980s in West European communist parties, in what was called the 'Eurocommunist' movement (Ross, 1991). Thus Santiago Carrillo (1977), at that time leader of the Spanish Communist Party, wrote that:

> The generations of Marxists who have lived through the grievous experience of Fascism and who, in another order of things, have experienced Stalinist degeneration, appraise the concept of democracy in a different way [from Lenin], and not in opposition to socialism and communism, but as a road towards them and *as a main component of them*. (p. 90)

and further:

> As regards the political system established in Western Europe, based on representative political institutions – parliament, political and philosophical pluralism, the theory of the separation of powers, decentralization, human rights, etc. – that system is in essentials valid and it will be still more effective with a socialist, and not a capitalist, economic foundation. (p. 105)

In a different context, the issue of civil and political rights has also become increasingly prominent in the Western democracies. One well-known instance is the civil rights movement of black Americans in the 1960s; and similar movements, involving various ethnic and cultural groups, continue to be active in many countries, as do women's movements. More generally, there is a growing debate about the effective exercise of civil and political rights within the present constitutional arrangements in some countries; and in Britain, for example, the movement known as Charter 88 has raised major issues concerning the reform of the electoral system, a written constitution and a bill of rights.

Secondly, the idea of social rights as a basic element in democratic citizenship, which was enshrined in the postwar welfare state, is increasingly a focus of political controversy and conflict in two respects. In the first place it is associated, as I have noted, with a general movement towards greater equality, and is contested by those social theorists of the New Right (King, 1987) who, in recent years, have criticized what they refer to as a 'dependency culture', and have urged instead the creation or restoration of an 'enterprise culture' of a more individualistic kind, in which the role of the state and other public authorities in providing welfare services would be radically diminished. This opposition – most vigorous in Britain and the US – to the extension of social rights as an essential feature of democracy will be considered more fully later (see Chapter 6), together with various countervailing movements which have found expression in the modest proposals of the European Community for a 'social charter', and increasingly in the demands of new socialist parties and allied groups in the East European countries for the safeguarding of those important rights which had been established by the former regimes.

The second major respect in which the assertion of the social rights of citizens has become more important is that it expresses the claims of very diverse groups in society to equal treatment, and at the same time broadens considerably the range of what are to be regarded as social rights. Not only the inequalities of class, but the kinds of deprivation experienced by particular groups or categories of the population – by ethnic or cultural groups, women, immigrants, the unemployed, the very poor, the homeless and others – now occupy a prominent place in political controversy and in the studies undertaken by social scientists. These new political ideas and researches have also stimulated debate about the scope of social rights, especially in the prosperous industrial countries, but also, in quite different circumstances, in poorer developing countries, where conceptions of 'development' itself have to be reconsidered in a new context. The question posed is how far social rights should now be conceived as including, beyond such things as education, health care and the alleviation of severe poverty, a right to employment or to an appropriate basic income, to decent housing, or to participation by employees in the management of their firms; and if they are so conceived, what policies and institutional changes could effectively establish them. In a somewhat different sense, involving to some extent the balance of rights between generations, the natural environment of human life and more generally the 'quality of life', has become a more prominent issue in relation both to economic development and to population growth, through the rapidly expanding activities of ecology movements.

The idea of democratic citizenship as involving a substantial and growing body of civil, political and social rights has thus, in the ways I have indicated, become a central theme in recent political thought about democracy. In the following chapters, and particularly in discussing recent social movements and political trends in the late twentieth century, I shall explore its further implications.

2 Social Movements, Parties and Political Action

In analyzing political action – that is to say, struggles for power – we need to look primarily at the activities of social groups rather than the actions of individuals, although the influence of particular individuals may evidently be a significant factor in some historical situations. A preliminary step in this analysis is to distinguish the various ways in which social groups may engage in politics, and the nature of the groups involved. Clearly, there is very great diversity, ranging from sporadic protests, riots and rebellions or *coups d'état*, to the more continuous activities of organized political parties, but most of these phenomena can, I think, be subsumed under two broad categories which I shall refer to as 'social movements' and 'organized political formations'.

Since the 1960s, when a number of new social movements – among them the student movement, various national and ethnic movements, and the women's movement – became extremely active in political life, a great deal more attention has been given by sociologists to such forms of political action, which may be seen not only as constituting a basis or context for the development of more highly organized political activities, but also as political forces in their own right, existing alongside and sometimes in conflict with, established parties and pressure groups. We may define a social movement, in broad terms, as a collective endeavour to promote or resist change in the society of which it forms part;[1] but this statement needs to be qualified in some way if we are to retain a clear distinction between a 'movement' and a 'party'. One way of doing this is to point out the less organized character of a movement, in which there may be no regular or easily identifiable membership (no 'party card' or dues), and little in the way of a central office or staff. Belonging to a movement is more a matter of sympathizing with a particular social outlook or doctrine, expressing it in everyday political debate and being ready to participate in occasional activities such as demonstrations or 'riotous assemblies'. Nevertheless, as social movements have developed in modern societies some of them have tended to become more organized, with a formal membership and an administrative staff. They can, however, still be distinguished from organized political formations such as parties which are directly engaged in the struggle for power in the sense of seeking to retain or capture the government of some political unit, by the fact that social movements act in a more diffuse way and if they are successful establish only the preconditions for changes of policy or regime by bringing into question the legitimacy of the existing political system (in part or in whole), creating a different climate of opinion, and proposing alternatives.

The distinction between a movement and a party, or other organized group, is shown also by the fact that large-scale movements tend to produce within themselves a variety of more or less directly political groups, as did the nineteenth-century labour movement; and the subsequent course of political action has then to be understood partly in terms of the relation between the broader movement and the various organized groups. In Marxist thought and practice this relation is posed as one between class and party, and it has been a matter of controversy since the end of the nineteenth century, expressed in the most diverse forms, extending from Michels' reflections upon the 'iron law of oligarchy' to Lenin's conception of the Bolshevik Party, theoretically elaborated by Lukács.[2]

Having established a distinction between social movements and organized political formations, and indicated in a preliminary way the characteristics of social movements, it would not be too difficult to construct a typology of such movements, as a number of writers have attempted,[3] in terms of their size (number of participants), range (local, national, international), duration, objectives (specific or general, directed toward transforming individuals or supra-individual systems) and so on.[4] But although such classifications may sometimes be useful in guiding empirical research they do not seem to me to take up directly the most important questions, which are those concerning the significance of social movements in the process of reproduction and transformation of total social systems. They do not, that is to say, make a very large contribution to a theory of social movements.

In order to understand how such a theory might be constructed we should begin by recognizing that social movements are essentially a phenomenon of modern societies. The term itself only began to be generally used in the early nineteenth century in Western Europe, and one of the first systematic discussions is to be found in the book by Lorenz von Stein,[5] where the social movement is portrayed as a struggle for greater social independence culminating in the class struggle of the proletariat. Stein's book may have influenced the initial formulation of Marx's conception of the proletariat in capitalist society (Avineri, 1972, pp. 53–5), but whether that is so or not it did undoubtedly express in a very clear and forceful way ideas which were widely held about the dominant political issues in nineteenth-century European societies; to such an extent that the social movement came to be largely identified, especially in Germany, with the labour movement. Of course, the identification was not complete, for as we have seen, Tocqueville attached greater importance to the democratic movement, animated and sustained by the middle class rather than the working class; but the labour movement was itself represented by its adherents as a prolongation of the democratic movement.

Beyond any such differences of interpretation, in any case, there was a common recognition that in one form or another large numbers of people in the post-revolutionary societies of Europe and North America had begun to take part actively and consciously in the construction and reconstruction of their societies. We can describe this historical situation as the beginning of an era of mass movements, among which, in the latter part of the nineteenth century, the labour movement appeared as the paradigm of a social movement. From this time, at first in Europe and North America, and subsequently in the rest of the world, a great number of social movements developed – nationalist movements in Central and Southeastern Europe, and later in colonial territories; women's movements which were concerned initially with the right to vote; youth movements; and a host of smaller, more sectional movements advocating particular causes – while the labour movement continued to advance and engendered a variety of new organizations on a national and international scale.

It is on the basis of this historical experience of modern social movements, and with the aid of concepts which were introduced in order to understand them, that social scientists and historians have gone on to study movements of a similar kind in other societies and periods; for example, millenarian movements,[6] peasant rebellions,[7] the actions of 'crowds' and 'mobs'.[8] The value of such studies is that they show plainly the ubiquity of popular political action, which may be diffuse, episodic, lacking any clearly formulated doctrine, or expressing itself mainly in religious or cultural terms, but always provides a matrix from which political organizations can emerge in favourable circumstances.

Nevertheless, the gap between movements of this kind (which have sometimes been called 'pre-political') and modern social movements remains large, for the latter exist on a vastly greater scale, are more directly involved in political conflict, are influenced by more rigorous and elaborate ideologies, and have as a rule a more enduring, less ephemeral, character. Their specific significance is that they form a crucial element in what has been called the 'self-production' of modern societies. According to this conception societies have now come to recognize themselves 'as the result of a social action, of decisions or transactions, of domination or conflicts' (Touraine, 1977, p. 1). In this process of self-creation social movements are the forces which contest an established system of historical action and seek to divert the development of society into a different channel.[9]

This idea of the innovative power of movements obviously owes a great deal to the events of the 1960s when there appeared quite suddenly large-scale movements expressing profound discontent with, and opposition to, the existing social and political order. These followed two decades of consolidation of the 'stable democracies' in the Western capitalist world, and of the presumably 'stable autocracies' in the socialist world of Eastern Europe, as well as the emergence of a 'Third World' (including many newly independent states) which was conceived by most Western political scientists as having embarked upon a process of gradual 'modernization' and 'industrialization'. The leading element in this upheaval was the student movement, and although students became independently active in political life all over the world – in Eastern Europe and in the Third World just as much as in the West – the principal expression of a distinctive radical doctrine and mode of political action, which became to a large extent a model for the whole international movement, was to be found in the US, in the Students for a Democratic Society (SDS).[10]

SDS began modestly in 1959 as the revived youth section of the old League for Industrial Democracy, but it soon began to grow as part of a general renaissance of radical ideas and movements in the New Left, and more particularly through the participation of students in the civil rights movement. Its first manifesto, the 'Port Huron Statement', launched the idea of 'participatory democracy', which was translated into political practice first in community action projects and subsequently in various forms of direct action in the universities (beginning with the Berkeley Free Speech Movement of 1964) and against the Vietnam war. The membership of SDS grew rapidly from about 4000 in 1965 to some 100,000 three years later, and throughout this period it had much larger numbers of supporters who identified themselves in some way with 'the Movement'.

The peak of the student movement, in Europe as well as in the US, was reached in 1968, marked most dramatically by the May revolt of the French students, which was supported briefly by a large part of the working-class movement.[11] Thereafter, the movement began to decline almost everywhere, largely as a result of repressive measures, which included such actions as the Soviet military occupation of Czechoslovakia, de Gaulle's threat to use the French army in a full-scale civil war, and a general harassment of radicals, particularly in the US and in West Germany. It was not only the student movement that suffered in this way; the black movement in the US, especially when it took a revolutionary form in the Black Panther Party, was violently suppressed, and in Latin America democratic and radical movements were destroyed, and military dictatorships were installed, often with American help, as in Chile.

Like the labour movement in its formative period – like Chartism, or the early trade unions, or the utopian communities – the social movements of the 1960s were movements of liberation seeking an adequate doctrine and mode of political action to combat the most oppressive features of the societies in which they developed; thus they directed their activities variously against colonial rule, domination by external economic powers, the rule of feudal-military elites, ethnic subordination, the subjection of women, or the domination of society by a rigid, centralized and bureaucratic apparatus. In the early 1970s some of these movements began to decline or were suppressed, but others continued to flourish. The anti-nuclear movement grew throughout the 1980s; nationalist and separatist movements have revived, for example in Scotland and Québec; the women's movement has had an increasing influence, although it is still far from accomplishing its larger aims; and ecology movements have become widespread and more influential. In Eastern Europe the opposition movements which began to grow rapidly in the 1980s were finally successful in bringing about the collapse of the communist regimes, but they have not yet been able to create an acceptable and stable new order; nationalist movements have proliferated, and a new labour movement has emerged which contests the policy of restoring free-market capitalism that has so far produced only economic disaster.

In the Western societies there seems to be little inclination at present to embark upon fresh experiments in political action on the scale of the 1960s. The 'self-production' of society, involving the mass participation of its members, is a complex and difficult undertaking, which perhaps requires a more buoyant and optimistic mood than now prevails. The rapid development of social movements during the 1960s depended in part upon sustained economic growth, full employment, the expansion of higher education, and a general feeling that these societies had entered what was often called a 'post-scarcity' era in which the fundamental problems of production had been solved and the conditions created for the development of a new society of leisure and enjoyment. This faith in affluence has now waned; there is a more profound concern about the use of natural resources and increasing scepticism about the prospects, as well as the consequences, of unlimited economic growth, in a period of economic depression and high unemployment.

The long-term success of social movements depends also upon several general conditions. In the first place, it is essential that such movements should formulate a doctrine which is capable of arousing sufficient enthusiasm and commitment to sustain political activity over a period of time. The doctrine, which may be concerned with national liberation, the emancipation of a class, the emancipation of women or some other general aim which is felt to be important by large numbers of people, has also to include or be founded upon a social theory which can elucidate the principal issues, clarify the objectives and ways of attaining them, and outline alternative forms of society. It was along this path that the labour movement, and within a narrower framework, nationalist movements, developed in the nineteenth century. The social movements of the 1960s were relatively unsuccessful in producing such doctrines in a coherent form; and the student movement, in particular, came to an end in a welter of conflicting views about the agencies and objectives of radical social change, beset by arguments about its own relation to the working-class movement, about the importance of cultural as against economic and structural changes in society, and about the role of violence in movements for social change. The black movement in the US was also divided, not only about its relationship with white radicalism, and about the use of violence, but also more fundamentally about whether its ultimate objective should be full assimilation into American society on equal terms with other ethnic groups or some form of separation and independence (Cruse, 1967).

There is a second important requirement for the success of a social movement. At some point in its development it has to create more organized political groups, or convert or capture existing political organizations, which are able to engage directly in a struggle for power and have the capacity to use power when they have gained it in order to reconstruct society. Many of the movements in the 1960s were reluctant to take this step, largely because of their hostility to the bureaucratic character of traditional parties, and they seem to have formed no clear idea of how the desired transformation of the economy, the political system and cultural patterns (including education) could actually be carried out in an effective way. Frequently, they expressed a sympathy for guerrilla activities and direct action, without recognizing that successful guerrilla movements were either controlled by an organized and disciplined party (as in China) or turned themselves into a traditional type of party (as in Cuba) when it became necessary to consolidate their rule and implement their policies. In many Third World countries national liberation movements which failed to create effective political parties were either taken over by military elites or else the governments which they formed were overthrown by military coups.[12] On the other hand, nationalist movements within industrial countries have had some success when they have been able to establish strong party organizations, as in the case of the Scottish National Party or the Parti Québecois, or more recently in the Soviet Union and Yugoslavia.

While many of those who were active in the social movements of the 1960s were distrustful of parties, and in some cases viewed society – an ideal society – as an unending process of imaginative creative activity, without any permanently established institutions, those who were deeply engaged in party politics were often inclined to regard the movements as merely disruptive and irresponsible. In those societies of the late twentieth century in which there exists at least a minimal freedom of expression and association social movements are a means by which members of society can express dissent and opposition in a direct and immediate way, and can challenge the indifference, remoteness or negligence of party machines. Parties, on the other hand, are the indispensable means for achieving or retaining power and thus for being able to implement and administer, over long periods, complex social policies.

Between these two forms of political action there is a perpetual tension, the nature of which will become clearer when we have examined the development of parties themselves. Like social movements, political parties are a modern phenomenon.[13] They came into existence along with democracy – with the development of parliaments and elections – after the American and French Revolutions, and were at first 'parties of notables', that is to say, relatively small electoral committees composed of individuals who had prestige and wealth in their own constituency or electoral district. With the gradual extension of the franchise, and the growing powers of elected assemblies, parties acquired a more permanent organization, on a national scale; but the next major development came only toward the end of the nineteenth century, with the advent of labour and socialist parties (first in Germany and Austria) which aimed to recruit a mass membership, not only as a way of financing election campaigns and other activities, but also as a means of political education and involvement. From this time the permanent mass party became the dominant factor in the politics of Western capitalist societies, and during the twentieth century it has spread throughout the rest of the world, though in diverse forms. It is important to distinguish the various ways in which mass parties were created. In the case of socialist parties, which gave the original impetus, the party was very largely an extension of an existing mass movement into the sphere of electoral politics, whereas conservative and liberal parties, which already had a strong representation in parliament and government, created their mass organization mainly from above, under the control of the parliamentary leaders.[14]

These divergent courses of development embodied different conceptions of politics and of political institutions. The socialist parties thought of themselves as the avant-garde of a class which was striving to bring into existence a new kind of society, and for them the struggle for power of the working class was, in principle, more important than any existing institutions. From this perspective, electoral politics were only one aspect of the struggle, and the parliamentary leaders were considered subordinate to the leadership of the mass party, which was at the same time the leadership of the class itself. Conservative and liberal parties, however much they in fact represented class interests, saw themselves as parties functioning within an established social order and a system of political institutions in which parliament was supreme. Hence the parliamentary leaders dominated the mass party, which was conceived only as a means for contesting elections.

The socialist conception of a party was very clearly expressed in the early development of the German Social Democratic Party (SDP). The political situation in Germany before 1914, in which parties had no direct role in the formation of the Imperial Government, which functioned independently of them, meant that the SPD had no reason to think of its activities mainly in parliamentary terms. Instead, it grew rapidly, after the period of illegality from 1878–90, as a mass party (with more than 1 million members by 1914) outside the existing political system, engaged in what Nettl (1965) called 'non-participating opposition', and by 1911 it had acquired 'all the appearance of a state within a state'. At this time it was, to use Nettl's term, an 'inheritor party'; that is to say, a party which expects to inherit power following the decline and overthrow of the existing political system and its socio-economic basis. Not only have many such parties appeared on the scene during the present century – the communist parties and anti-colonial parties

such as the Indian National Congress [15] – but there is in all socialist parties
(as well as in some right-wing parties, such as the fascist parties of the
1920s) a persistent element of non-participating opposition. Thus, one
of the major criticisms formulated by the social movements of the
1960s, and by radical groups within socialist and labour parties, was
directed against 'consensus politics' which placed a high value upon the
existing parliamentary institutions and played down the commitment
to radical changes in the social system.

This distinction corresponds, to some extent, with that between
'reformist' and 'revolutionary' parties, the former being concerned to
accommodate unavoidable changes (if they are more conservative) or
to bring about desirable changes (if they are more radical) within an
existing social and political order which is broadly accepted, while the
latter aim to establish a new order. In this sense all socialist parties are
revolutionary, since their objective is to replace a capitalist form of society
by a socialist one; so also are nationalist parties which seek to overthrow
colonial rule, and perhaps in a more limited sense right-wing parties,
such as fascist parties, which attempt to restore a more hierarchical and
authoritarian type of society. The characteristics of revolutionary, as
against reformist, parties have, of course, often been held to include,
besides this ambition to create a wholly new social order, a commitment
to rapid and violent social change. But these aspects, it seems to me, are
less fundamental. There is no contradiction in terms in referring to a
'slow revolution', as Otto Bauer did, or to a peaceful and democratic
revolution, as many socialists have done. The rate at which social
change is accomplished and the role of violence in political life raise
questions which are conceptually distinct from that of revolutionary
change and need to be examined independently.

Even if we confine ourselves to the difference of aim between
reformist and revolutionary parties (or of social movements, which can
be classified in a similar way), the distinction cannot always be made in
an absolutely clear-cut fashion. An accumulation of reforms may in fact
bring into existence a very different kind of society,[16] and reformist parties
may be led, by circumstances and by their responses to them, into
advocating and implementing more substantial changes in society than
they had originally envisaged. On the other side, revolutionary parties
may come to accept more of the existing social institutions than they
did in their first enthusiastic advocacy of a brave new world. Something
of the kind seems to have happened in the case of the European
communist parties; thus Santiago Carrillo (1977), in the passage quoted

earlier, says plainly that 'the political system established in Western Europe ... is in essentials valid', and this is far removed from the outlook of some earlier Marxists – and of the members of a few left-wing groupuscules even today – who talk about 'smashing the bourgeois state'.

But although the distinction between reformist and revolutionary parties may thus become somewhat blurred – and the sharpness of the distinction is further diminished by the difficulty of determining precisely what is to count as a fundamental change in a social system – it remains an important one, compared with which many other distinctions that have been made between parties, and between party systems, seem less significant. Thus the distinction between one-party systems and multi-party systems is to a great extent only an aspect of the differences we have just considered, for one-party or 'one-dominant party'[17] regimes are generally the creation of 'inheritor parties', either socialist or nationalist. Within the category of multi-party systems, whose existence is connected with modern Western democracy, a further distinction can be made between those in which there are two dominant parties (with only weak third parties) and those in which there are several parties, each having substantial support. But this distinction is also far from being precise. There are important third parties in some two-party systems (the Liberal Democrats in Britain, the FDP in Germany, the New Democratic Party in Canada), and in federal states there may be considerable differences between the parties which are most prominent in national elections and those which have considerable support at the state or provincial level, as has often been the case in Canada. Furthermore, a two-party system may come to resemble a system with several parties if each of the parties involved is itself a relatively loose assemblage of diverse groups without strict voting discipline, and on the other side, in regimes with several parties, electoral alliances may bring about a situation which is close to a two-party system, as has been the case in France in recent years.

The diversity of party systems in the Western democracies is an outcome of social, cultural and historical influences, and of electoral systems themselves. So far as the latter are concerned it has often been noted that a simple-majority single ballot system tends to produce a two-party system, proportional representation a system with several parties, and a simple majority two-ballot system a regime in which there are several parties, but the formation of electoral alliances may result in something like a two-party system. It would be better to say perhaps that electoral systems reinforce existing tendencies, because such systems are themselves the product of diverse constellations of political interests and parties, and of changes in those constellations. Thus two-party systems in the twentieth century became established where there was a clear division between two major classes (Britain providing a good example), whereas systems with several parties have emerged in conditions where such class divisions were complicated by religious differences, by the existence of a significantly large peasantry, by divisions in the working-class movement between socialist and communist parties, and by a variety of other cultural factors and historical legacies.[17]

These circumstances are themselves historically changing, and in response to the changes new social movements and parties may emerge within the established political system, as did the socialist parties, and later the communist and fascist parties, in Europe. The success or failure of such third parties, or more generally of new parties, is affected by many social factors, as well as by the political system itself, including the electoral system. In the US, for example, where the socialist party failed to establish itself as a major party after a fairly rapid growth in the first decade of this century, it has long been argued that the presidential system is a major obstacle to the development of third parties,[18] and undoubtedly these constitutional factors have been important; but it is clear that many other social and economic characteristics of the US have had a preponderant influence in determining the absence of a large-scale independent socialist movement or party there (Sombart, 1906; Laslett and Lipset, 1974). In some European countries with a two-party system, in which the parties have traditionally been closely associated with the major classes in capitalist society, changes in the class structure – such as were examined in Chapter 1 – have made possible the emergence or revival of 'centre' parties, and changes of this kind may in due course have an impact upon the electoral system itself. In Britain, for example, there is at the present time a vigorous controversy about the introduction of proportional representation, stoutly resisted by the two main parties, but supported by a growing part of the population who have become increasingly dissatisfied with the existing system, which produces a gross discrepancy between the votes cast for various parties and their representation in parliament, and results in practice in a form of minority government.

The foregoing discussion suggests that political parties can be regarded in two different ways. They are, as I have emphasized, highly organized political formations, which tend to develop a life of their own, to some extent independent of the social interests that originally gave rise to them and of their changing environment, and may acquire the character (or at least the appearance) of permanent elements in the political system. Social democratic parties have existed in Europe for a century or more; the Democratic and Republican parties in the US are well over a century old, and indeed have a certain continuity with earlier parties dating from the time of the American Revolution; conservative parties on a mass basis were created soon after the emergence of social democracy in Europe; and communist parties were formed on a world scale after the Russian Revolution. It was this aspect which engaged the attention of Michels (1911), in his study of socialist parties (and especially the German Social Democratic Party), in which he argued that the party becomes personified in the full-time paid officials – the bureaucracy and parliamentary leaders – whose interests may diverge from those of the mass membership and still more from the wider group which the party claims to represent, and who have an overwhelming influence upon party policy.

At the same time, however, it should be recognized that not all parties retain their vitality, or even survive at all, that new parties emerge, and may quickly become powerful, as happened with the socialist parties in Europe, and that parties may change their character and their policies without necessarily changing their names. In some measure at least, the immutability of parties and party systems seems to be an illusion which results simply from taking an unhistorical view. Leaving aside the numerous examples of the rise and fall of parties over the past century, there are many instances of change even in the relatively short period of time since the end of the Second World War. Especially in the 'new nations', political parties which emerged from the independence movements have either consolidated their position, or have been challenged and replaced by still newer parties, or destroyed by military coups. In the older nation states, after the war, fascist parties disappeared (although they have begun to re-emerge on a small scale in recent years), regional and nationalist parties have been formed within existing states, there has been a succession of new political parties (and destruction of them by military intervention) in Latin America, while in some European countries there has been a revival of liberal and 'centre' parties and the emergence of 'green' parties. Even where there has been continuity in party organization changes of orientation have occurred. In Eastern Europe since 1990 the old communist parties have largely disappeared, but new socialist and labour parties are beginning to emerge; and many West European communist parties have also reconstituted themselves, under different names, as social democratic parties.

The impression gained from observing the political events of the present century is not one of great stability and permanence, but rather of considerable turbulence and changeability in the organization and expression of political interests. Of course, political parties do provide an important element of continuity, much more so in some countries than in others, but everywhere they are very much open to the influence of changing economic conditions, changes in the composition of society in terms of classes, social strata and interest groups, and new cultural orientations. It is here that the importance of social movements becomes apparent, for such movements – whether they are large-scale and enduring, like the trade union movement, or more specific, concerned with particular issues in some historical period, like the unemployed workers' movements of the 1930s – do not only establish, in some cases, the preconditions for the emergence or transformation of organized political formations, but also constitute an independent form of political commitment and action which is an essential, often highly effective, element in political struggles. Piven and Cloward (1977), for example, in their admirable study of four lower-class protest movements in the US,[19] attribute greater effectiveness to mass protests than to the efforts to build mass-based permanent organizations: 'Whatever influence lower-class groups occasionally exert in American politics does not result from organization, but from mass protest and the disruptive consequences of protest' (p. 36). A similar view of the importance of social movements is taken by Touraine (1973) in his account of the Popular Unity Government of Salvador Allende in Chile where, he argues, the activities and influence of a variety of movements within the governing coalition made it possible for the poor to express their grievances directly and continuously, instead of having them diverted (and perhaps stifled) in the official channels of a monolithic ruling party.

What is perhaps most striking in the past three decades is the way in which social movements of very diverse kinds have become an accepted part of political life in the Western democracies, and to some extent have provided models for movements in countries where the expression of criticism, dissent and opposition through formal political institutions is virtually impossible. In a somewhat schematic way it is possible, I think, to distinguish three main phases in the development of modern social movements. The first is that in which movements such as the democratic movement and the labour movement in Europe, the women's suffrage movement and independence movements in colonial territories at a later time, or present-day movements in autocratic states, provide the only effective means for expressing grievances and seeking to bring about political changes. A second stage emerges when the achievement of representative government, universal and equal suffrage, and free elections seems to diminish the importance of political action outside the formal institutional sphere, although in periods of crisis social movements, such as the unemployed workers' movements or the fascist movements in some European countries, may develop. The third, present stage in the Western democracies seems to me one in which there is a considerable revival and proliferation of social movements as a more or less permanent feature of political life, reflecting a broader movement to extend democracy. Representative government, parties and elections are now seen increasingly as providing an essential framework but as inadequate by themselves to establish a democratic society in the more radical sense of government *by* the people.

The general regulation of economic and social life at the national level, and relations with other nation states, require a complex apparatus of government and administration, parties with broadly formulated aims and policies, and competition between parties; but there is also a need for more direct and immediate means of political action, which would allow the effective expression of particular grievances and interests, counter some of the consequences of centralization and bureaucratic administration and make possible a more continuous practical participation by large numbers of citizens in determining the quality of their lives. Another way of stating this point would be to say that the revival and growth of social movements in those societies which are both economically advanced and have a fairly long tradition of democracy, is a major aspect of that 'self-production' of society referred to earlier, which exists in some degree already, but is still more an ideal representation of a future form of society, 'free of domination', in which the collectivity would really govern itself, by procedures of rational discussion among equal citizens.

How far present-day societies are likely to proceed along this road is a matter of debate (and I shall return to the question in Chapter 6), but at the least it has to be recognized that in recent years the idea of political action has been very substantially broadened, so that there is already a quite widespread awareness of the variety of ways in which individuals and groups of individuals can assert their dissent from the policies of government at all levels (for example, the revolt against the poll tax in Britain) and bring into the arena of public debate alternative policies.

3   Types of Political System

Classifications of political systems have been undertaken in diverse ways and for a variety of purposes. From the point of view of a science of politics classification can be seen as an elementary form of theory construction which involves the kind of generalization required in order to assign phenomena to particular classes.[1] As such it needs to make use of concepts which define the political sphere, the nature of political relations and institutions, the state, government, law, etc.; and it generally has as its point of departure a broader scheme of thought about human nature and society. Many of the classifications that were proposed in the nineteenth century rested upon a conception of social evolution, which itself was understood in various ways and was frequently connected with the idea of progress. Other distinctions that were drawn – between democracy and absolutism, between monarchy and republic, between Western political institutions and 'Oriental despotism' – expressed current political interests and ideological commitments; and indeed all the attempts to construct a typology of political systems are marked to some degree by an intermingling of scientific analysis and the value judgements which arise from real political struggles.

This does not mean, however, that the scientific and ideological elements cannot be distinguished; and a further distinction may be made between those classifications which are more descriptive and those which have a larger theoretical content. Political scientists who were, or are, little influenced by sociology have produced classifications which are mainly descriptive, dividing political regimes, for example, into monarchies and republics, federal and unitary states. For political sociology, on the other hand, the principal question is the relation between a form of society and a type of political system; and from this point of view the foregoing distinctions may have little significance. Modern attempts to classify political regimes have begun for the most part from some general theory of society, and as I have indicated they were strongly influenced at the outset (and again in recent decades) by conceptions of social evolution or development.

We may take as quite different examples of such endeavours the theories of Spencer and Marx. Although Spencer worked out an elaborate scheme of social evolution, in terms of the increasing scale and complexity of societies, his political sociology was based mainly upon a fairly simple distinction between 'militant' and 'industrial' societies, the former being characterized by the predominance of activities concerned with defence and offence (that is, warfare), the latter by the predominance of activities concerned with 'sustentation' (that is, production and trade). In the industrial type of society there is, according to Spencer, a tendency for central regulation and coercive control to decline and to be replaced by representative institutions and a more diffuse system of regulation; but this view is then qualified in various ways, and Spencer finally concludes that representative government depends largely upon the existence of a particular type of economy – the *laissez-faire* free-enterprise economy – which creates the conditions in which 'multitudinous objects are achieved by spontaneously evolved combinations of citizens governed representatively'. This idea of a connection between the capitalist economy and a democratic political system appeared in various forms in accounts of the transition that was seen as occurring in the nineteenth-century European societies (for example, as a movement from status to contract, or from authority to citizenship), and it has continued to have an important influence in political theory to the present day. Similarly, the notion of social development through increasing differentiation and individuation has had a considerable place in later sociological theories, although its political implications have been judged in diverse ways; from one aspect social differentiation may be seen as creating a mutual dependence of individuals and groups which is a fundamental element in a stable democratic system, while from another aspect (as in Durkheim's theory) it may be regarded as a danger to the political order if it leads to excessive individualism, and then needs to be checked by a moral consensus embodied in the state.

Social development, in Spencer's conception, forms part of an all-embracing process of cosmic evolution, and it is treated in a very abstract and schematic way. Marx's theory, on the contrary, deals directly with the actual history of societies, draws upon historical studies and poses historical problems. The basis of his account of social development is the distinction between different economic structures or modes of production – comprising 'forces', or technical means, of production and 'social relations' of production, which include the distribution of the means of production (property) and of the product, as well as the social division of labour – to which different forms of society and the state correspond. In Marx's (1859, Preface) own concise formulation of his theory of history:

> The mode of production of material life determines the general character of the social, political, and spiritual process of life…. In broad outline we can designate the Asiatic, the ancient, the feudal, and the modern bourgeois modes of production as progressive epochs in the economic formation of society.

Earlier, in the first systematic exposition of his new conception, Marx (Marx and Engels, 1845–6) indicated four stages of development in the division of labour and the forms of property, in European societies, from tribal property to the communal and state property of antiquity, then to feudal or estates property, and finally to modern capitalist property. In the *Grundrisse* manuscript of 1857–8,[2] Marx discussed social development in greater detail, on the basis of a wider historical knowledge which is no longer confined to Europe; it is in this work that the concept of 'Asiatic society' is introduced, and as Hobsbawm (1964, p. 32) remarked there now seem to be three or four alternative routes out of the primitive communal system: the oriental, the ancient, the Germanic (or more broadly, feudal), and less clearly articulated, the Slavonic. Marx himself, as is well known, devoted the greater part of his historical studies to the development of modern capitalism; his knowledge of some other forms of society was limited, especially in the case of primitive communal society which he began to study systematically only in the years 1879–82, after the publication of L. H. Morgan's *Ancient Society*.[3]

Thus Marx's model of historical development was in many respects only a sketch which left many problems unresolved. Four issues stand out as being of crucial importance: how many distinct 'modes of production' are there; in what order do these modes of production succeed each other and how is their sequence to be explained; what forms of society necessarily correspond with, arise from, or are determined by the different modes of production; and lastly, what are the forms of state, or political systems, that are characteristic of, or produced by, different economic structures and forms of society? It can scarcely be claimed that these questions have yet been answered in such a manner as to transform Marx's very general model into a systematic and well-supported theory of historical development. Nevertheless, the model has inspired much detailed historical research – indeed it has contributed substantially to the progress of economic and social history – and in the past few decades, partly as a result of the publication of previously inaccessible manuscripts of Marx, there have been some valuable contributions to Marxist scholarship addressed to the kinds of problem that I have indicated, concerning modes of production,[4] tribal (that is, primitive communal) societies,[5] historical sequences,[6] and the relation of political power to forms of society.[7]

In these recent studies the idea of a unilinear development of society has been largely abandoned, even as representing the view of Marx himself, and it is argued instead that there are alternative forms of society which have succeeded the primitive communal system. One important distinction between these types of society is that some may be resistant to further development while others facilitate it, and thus a contrast is established between the development of society in Western Europe, through feudalism to capitalism, and the relative immutability of Asiatic societies. Further, it has been argued that there is no 'Asiatic mode of production', so that the distinctive history of the Orient has to be explained in terms of influences other than a specific mode of production; for instance, by the character and development of political or religious institutions. In the same way, the contrasting development of the Western European societies may also become comprehensible only as the outcome of distinctive political, religious or other forces working within a particular mode of production. Thus there is no world history, with clearly marked and universal stages of development, but only separate histories of different areas of the world; and we are led to a conception like that of Max Weber, in which the unique features in the history of Western Europe, and especially those which gave an impetus to the development of capitalism, are emphasized.[8]

There is a similar departure from the notion of a fixed sequence of modes of production and their corresponding political and cultural forms in recent works which concentrate their attention upon specific types of political regime which do not necessarily fall within a single time span. A good example is Anderson's study of the absolutist state in Europe, where it is observed that there is no 'uniform temporal medium: for the times of the major Absolutisms of Europe – Eastern and Western – were, precisely, enormously diverse.... The wide disjunctures in the dating of these great structures inevitably corresponded to deep distinctions in their composition and evolution' (1974b, p. 10). The historical problem becomes, not how to establish a sequence of political regimes associated with a universal process of socio-economic development, but how to explain the interconnection of different elements within a particular historical type of society and state. The principal distinction that Anderson makes is between capitalism and pre-capitalist social formations:

> Capitalism is the first mode of production in history in which the means whereby the surplus is pumped out of the direct producer is 'purely' economic in form.... All other previous modes of exploitation operate through *extra-economic* sanctions – kin, customary, religious, legal or political.... In consequence, pre-capitalist modes of production cannot be defined *except* via their political, legal and ideological superstructures.... A scrupulous and exact taxonomy of these legal and political configurations is thus a precondition of establishing any comprehensive typology of pre-capitalist modes of production. (pp. 403–4)

A similar conception, formulated in a more abstract manner, prevails in the work of the 'structuralist' Marxists; notably in Poulantzas' (1968) study of the capitalist state, where the object of enquiry – politics in capitalist social formations – is constituted by reference to a general concept of 'mode of production', defined as being composed of different levels (economic, political, ideological and theoretical) which form a complex whole determined, in the last instance, by the economic level, but in which the economic level does not necessarily have the dominant role. What distinguishes one mode of production from another is the particular articulation of the various levels or elements.

One prominent tendency in recent Marxist thought, therefore, has been to replace the relatively simple and precise evolutionary scheme of Marx's 1859 Preface by a more complex and indefinite picture of the history of society in which, beyond the primitive communal stage, two broad types of society are distinguished – pre-capitalist and capitalist – each of which may develop very diverse forms of economy, politics and culture. At the same time, the teleological elements in Marx's thought have been given up; there is no single line of development passing through necessary stages to the attainment of socialism. The breakdown of capitalism and the advent of a new form of society are conceived and explained as the outcome of the way a particular structure – the capitalist mode of production and capitalist society – works, not as the product of a historical process; and the post-capitalist societies which can be foreseen, or which actually exist, may be as varied as were feudal societies or the absolutist states. Furthermore, they may bear little resemblance to the ideological representations of socialism, strongly marked by teleology, in terms of the end of alienation or the overcoming of antagonistic forms of society.

This kind of analysis has implications for the Marxist theory of the state. It too can no longer be presented in a teleological form as an account of a historical process which begins with primitive 'stateless' societies, then passes through a definite sequence of class societies in which the state comes into existence and develops, and concludes with a higher form of communal society which is again 'stateless'. Instead, the theory has to relate types of state to distinct socio-economic structures, without placing them as a whole in any historical sequence, and to explain changes in the state by characteristics of the structure of each particular form of society which engender a structural transformation. But the theory still needs a general concept of the state, and this may be elaborated in such a way as to retain, covertly, the idea of 'stateless' societies existing at the beginning and end of a historical process. From a non-evolutionist standpoint, however, the problems that can be posed concerning the state, within a Marxist conception, are limited to the following: the formation of the state as a consequence of a structural transformation of primitive communal societies (so far as these can be properly located and studied); the types of state which correspond with determinate, historically realized, modes of production, and the conditions which produce a transition from one type to another; and in the case of capitalist society, the structural characteristics, including the contradictions, which may effect a transition to another (unknown) type of society. There is no place in such an analysis for the speculative concept of 'advanced communism' which belongs to the philosophy of history.

It is an entirely different question whether the Marxist concept of the state as the necessary product of the division of society into classes (which is also sufficient to produce it) is itself adequate, irrespective of whether or not it is incorporated into an evolutionist scheme. Two particular instances will illustrate some of the difficulties. Let us assume, in accordance with the Marxist concept, that in the earliest human societies there was no political domination, in however rudimentary a form (not even the domination of women by men), though this may seem less probable than it once did, in the light of recent studies of animal societies. The problem then is to explain how the state came to be formed historically, through the dissolution of the primitive communal group; and a broadly Marxist account of this process (leaving aside here the diverse interpretations and controversies among Marxist sociologists and anthropologists) rests essentially upon the conception of a change in the mode of production, involving a greater inequality of property, which itself is brought about by a development of the forces of production through technological progress. Marx, especially in his notes on Morgan, mentioned various factors, including conquest, as playing a part in the creation of the state, but without examining the influence of warfare and military organization as such,[9] or the consequences of the growing scale of societies.

These two elements are also important with respect to the second instance; namely, the character and development of the state in modern capitalist societies, and in the various forms of post-capitalist society. It is difficult, I think, with the experience of such societies in mind, to attribute a theoretical sense to the idea that a type of society will emerge in which the state and politics no longer exist. The size and complexity of advanced industrial societies, the diversity of interests within them, the need to administer vast enterprises engaged either in production or in the provision of transport, education, health services and so on, and international rivalries and conflicts, all point to a widening sphere of state activity in legislation, administration, the legal regulation of disputes among individuals and groups, and the promotion of what are seen as national interests. Political power may be decentralized to some extent, made more democratic, involve the active participation of larger numbers of people, become less directly coercive, but there seems to be no ground upon which to base a theory of the total 'withering away' of the state and the whole political sphere.

So far I have discussed two attempts to distinguish the different types of political system in terms of an evolutionary scheme; one of them (that of Spencer) being so abstract as to have little value in establishing a precise historical sequence, while the other (that of Marx) possesses less of an evolutionary character than may at first sight appear and leaves unsolved many problems in the construction of an adequate typology of pre-capitalist and capitalist societies. In the last few decades the interest shown by social scientists in such evolutionary schemes has waned, notwithstanding the growing attention paid to problems of 'development'; for the latter notion is not usually incorporated into any general conception of the history of human society, and despite first appearances is largely unhistorical. Development, or modernization, has been seen for the most part in terms of a simple distinction between 'traditional' and 'modern', 'underdeveloped' and 'developed', 'agrarian' and 'industrial' societies, in the context of the present time, or of very recent history.

In this respect, however, the distinctions that are made resemble many others in political science which, as I noted at the beginning of this chapter, frequently emerge out of the dominant political concerns of the age. Thus in eighteenth-century Europe the traditional typology of monarchy, oligarchy and democracy, originally formulated by the Greeks, was given a new sense in the writings of Montesquieu by the contrast between 'Oriental despotism' and the monarchies of Western Europe, which was further developed by Adam Smith, Hegel and later economists and historians, and played a considerable part in the formation of Marx's conception of the Asiatic mode of production; one main feature of the contrast being the 'progressiveness' of Western societies as against the 'immobility' of Asiatic societies.[10] In the nineteenth century, after the American and French revolutions, another distinction – between monarchy and republic – assumed great importance, and republicanism developed as a radical political movement directed against survivals or attempted restorations of the *ancien régime*, merging to a large extent with the general democratic movement. Later in the century, with the rise of the labour movement, a different contrast was drawn, between capitalism and socialism, between 'bourgeois democracy' and 'socialist democracy', and this distinction has largely dominated political controversy up to the present time. Nevertheless, in the course of the twentieth century, following the experience of various forms of dictatorship, some of which have developed from socialist revolutions, this distinction has been overlaid by another, between 'totalitarianism' and 'democracy', or as it is sometimes expressed, between one-party and multi-party systems.[11] A further contrast, as I have indicated, may be drawn between the political systems of 'developed' and 'underdeveloped' societies, often in terms of the instability of the latter as compared with the former (Huntington, 1968); an instability which manifests itself partly in the frequency of military coups and the prevalence of military regimes in the non-industrial countries.

Faced with the great variety of distinctions that I have indicated we may ask whether they can in fact be brought within the compass of a single typology. It is evident, at least, that this has not yet been achieved in any generally acceptable way, and in this sense some of the basic elements in the theoretical framework of political sociology remain indefinite. The evolutionist schemes are too abstract and simple to comprehend the diverse political systems which have emerged within the largely separate political histories of different regions of the world; and in spite of all the qualifications that have been introduced they are too closely bound up with the idea of progress – if not unilinear then at least converging upon the same end – to entertain the possibility that political systems might be repeated, *mutatis mutandis*, in the course of history: that new kinds of autocracy or new forms of empire might succeed democratic regimes.

This is not to say that absolutely no general trends are discernible in the development of political systems. In a long historical perspective, and more particularly since the rise of industrial capitalism, there has obviously been – accompanying the growth and internal differentiation of societies – an increase in the scale of government, in the degree of political intervention in the general conduct of social life and in organized political activity; a growth of bureaucratic administration; and the formation of a distinctive, now predominant type of political unit – the nation state. Furthermore, the twentieth century may be regarded from one aspect as the culminating stage in a process whereby the world has been transformed, not into a single political system, but into a single political arena in which there are no longer isolated and autonomous units, but all states and political movements are enmeshed in global politics within which they exhibit varying degrees of dependence or independence.

Before proceeding to consider whether a more satisfactory typology of political systems might now be constructed, it will be useful at this stage to examine somewhat more closely the ways in which the concepts 'state' and 'political system' are employed. Let me begin by stating more fully the view I have already intimated, that political activities – that is to say, struggles for power among individuals and groups in relation to their own interests and to the general regulation and orientation of collective life – occur in every human society. In this sense, therefore, every society has a political system – a body of rules and practices, however informal, rudimentary and unspecific, which constitutes the framework (itself subject to change) within which such struggles, involving confrontations between different possible courses of action, normally take place – and it seems to me entirely erroneous and misleading to speak, as some Marxists have done, about societies in which there is no 'political level'.

To say, however, that every society has a political system is not to assert that every society has a 'state', in the sense of possessing a quite distinct and separate political apparatus. 'Stateless societies' have existed, in which political conflicts and decisions are bound up with kinship relations, or with religious conceptions and rituals, and all or most adult members of society may participate in these activities, without any specialized group of people being able to claim a particular responsibility for carrying them on. This situation has been described by Southall (1968) (see also Middleton and Tait, 1958) as follows:

Stateless societies are so constituted that the kaleidoscopic succession of concrete social situations provides the stimulus that motivates each individual to act for his own interest or for that of close kin and neighbours with whom he is so totally involved, in a manner which maintains the fabric of society ... the lack of specialized roles and the resulting multiplex quality of social networks mean that neither economic nor political ends can be exclusively pursued by anyone to the detriment of society, because the ends are intertwined with each other and further channelled by ritual and controlled by the beliefs which ritual expresses.

Stateless societies are for the most part small tribal societies, without any complex division of labour and economically poor, but some features of their political systems may perhaps also be found in other types of society, especially in village communities such as those of medieval Germany, or of India (where they were once described as 'little republics'), although in these instances there is already some degree of subordination to a state, however remote, and some element of strat-ification and inequality of power in the local community itself. If we regard stateless tribal societies as being in some measure representative of very early human societies, we can then ask what causes have brought the state into existence and assured its further development. The answers to this question fall into two main categories. One kind of answer refers to the increasing differentiation of social functions as human societies become larger and more complex, and to the need for a superior authority in society capable of regulating conflicts of interest among individuals and groups and of representing in some fashion the 'general interest'. The alternative view is that the state comes into being and is maintained as an instrument of domination, as a result either of the internal differentiation of society into dominant and subordinate classes (according to the Marxist theory), or of the imposition of the rule of one group of people upon another by conquest (as Oppenheimer argued).

These two conceptions of the state provide a familiar antithesis in the history of political thought, and they are repeated in various forms, often tacitly conveyed, in modern political science. It does not seem to me necessary or desirable to adhere exclusively to one or other of these the-oretical positions. Exactly how and when the first state emerged in the history of human society is a problem impossible to resolve; and for that matter it is by no means inconceivable that embryonic forms of the state always existed as an inheritance from animal societies. At all events, the early history of societies reveals that war and conquest played an important part in the development of the state, not only by creating clearly defined dominant groups, but also by enlarging the scale of society, hence stimulating both a greater internal differentiation of functions, and the growth of a centralized apparatus of government and administration.

For most of human history political domination in the shape of empires, hereditary rulers, aristocracies, has been largely taken for granted, notwithstanding sporadic revolts, so that Mosca's (1896) observation that 'in all societies – from societies that are very meagrely developed and have barely attained the dawnings of civilization, down to the most advanced and peaceful societies – two classes appear – a class that rules and a class that is ruled', is no more than the recognition of a historical and, as he says, 'obvious' fact. Only in modern times, since the power of ruling groups was explicitly and widely challenged in the name of democracy, and later of social democracy, has the question of the nature and basis of the state become a matter of acute controversy, giving rise to the two antithetical conceptions which I have indicated. At the same time it is in the modern democratic societies that this sharp antithesis between the state as a system of domination and the state as a welfare system becomes increasingly dubious, and it becomes necessary to consider it from these two aspects simultaneously.

In the Western democracies of the late twentieth century the state has taken on an entirely different character from that which it had in the period of *laissez-faire* capitalism, or in earlier periods, when its functions were mainly confined to tax collecting, internal repression, and external conflict with other states; now it is responsible in addition for the operation of a great range of public services as well as a general regulation of the whole economic system. Among the developed industrial countries generally it was mainly in the former communist societies of Eastern Europe that the repressive functions of the state were still prominent against a similar background of economic planning and provision of welfare services. The world political order has also undergone a change with the disappearance of empires, even though various forms of more or less onerous political dependence and subordination remain.

Looking back from the vantage point of the twentieth-century 'welfare state' we can also see, however, that every state, even when it has had a primarily repressive character, has also performed other necessary functions in the coordination and regulation of complex societies, especially through the development of a system of law, and in some cases – as with the Roman Empire – has had a generally civilizing influence. Hence a view of the state which emphasizes its pre-eminent character as a system of domination may also recognize the need for some kind of organized public power in every society, and come to be concerned rather with the form of the state than with its mere existence. There is a suggestion of such an approach in Marx's briefly sketched political theory, not only in his early criticism of Hegel's philosophy of the state as revealing the 'imperfection of the modern state', its representation of an 'illusory general interest' as against a real general interest, but also in the later *Critique of the Gotha Programme* (1875), where he poses, but does not answer, the question 'what transformation will the state undergo in communist society ... what social functions will remain in existence there that are analogous to present state functions?' Such reflections, of course, are counterbalanced by equally sketchy references to the 'dictatorship of the proletariat' during the period of transition from capitalism to socialism, and to the eventual 'abolition of the state', the elimination of 'a political power properly so-called', and the replacement of 'the government of men by the administration of things' (the latter notion derived from Saint-Simon). These fragmentary observations – some of them, like the contrast between government and administration, misleading[12] – clearly do not amount to a systematic theory of the political transition from capitalist to socialist society, or of the eventual nature of a socialist political system. Only in recent years has there been a sustained attempt by Marxist thinkers to re-examine in a thoroughgoing fashion the relation between the state, the economy and social classes, or to analyze that historical experience which reveals the emergence of a new type of authoritarian state from the revolutionary process itself or from the centralized control of a socialist economy.[13]

There is another style of political sociology, much influenced by Marxism, which has emphasized just as strongly the nature of the state as a system of domination; namely, the elite theory of Pareto and Mosca. In this case, domination is regarded as a universal and ineradicable feature of human societies, explained either by innate differences among human beings (Pareto, 1915–19) or by the superior power which an organized minority always possesses in relation to the unorganized majority (Mosca, 1896), although in Mosca's work some concession is made to the view that the progress of democracy reduces the gap between rulers and ruled.[14] Max Weber's political sociology has a close affinity with the ideas of the elite theorists, especially Mosca, in its acceptance of the universality of domination, its emphasis upon the power of organized minorities, its addiction to nationalism, and its refusal to conceive any real possibility of ending, or even substantially limiting, domination through an extension of democracy.[15] Weber differed, however, in incorporating rather more of the Marxist analysis into his own theory, in so far as he recognized social classes – and more generally, various 'constellations of interest' in the economic sphere – as important bases of domination, in his intense preoccupation with the growth of bureaucratic domination, and in the concentration of his analysis upon the different ways in which domination can make claims to 'legitimacy' and so constitute itself as a moral authority.[16]

Weber's theoretical scheme, while it recognizes diverse 'social bases' of politics, in the manner of Marx (and also of Mosca), at the same time attributes a degree of autonomy to politics, and allows for a partly independent development of the state itself. Again, like Marx and the elite theorists he conceives the state largely, if not wholly, in terms of domination; and this 'realist' view[17] distinguishes him sharply from those social scientists who, while differing about what the role of the state should be (how interventionist or *laissez-faire*), agree fundamentally in regarding it as an autonomous and neutral body, which arbitrates among competing claims and expresses the real consensus in society that underlies particular conflicts of interest. As I have shown, the theory of the state as a system of domination, in its Marxist form, has been qualified and extensively revised in recent years, while the elite theories have also been obliged to confront, however inadequately, the possibility that domination becomes a less salient characteristic with the growth of democracy.

It is rather more doubtful whether there has been any substantial revision of the opposed theory, of the state as a welfare system and an authentic embodiment of the 'general will', in order to take account of real inequalities of political power or the existence, throughout history, of evidently repressive regimes. Thus one well-known recent exponent of this theory, Talcott Parsons (1969, chap. 14), wrote in his analysis of the concept of political power that: 'Power, then, is generalized capacity to secure the performance of binding obligations by units in a system of collective organization when the obligations are legitimized with reference to their bearing on collective goals'. In this definition, and throughout Parsons' analysis, 'power' is identified with 'legitimate authority', and this authority itself is assumed to arise from some kind of pervasive agreement upon the collective purposes of society as a whole. This view is close to, and was influenced by, Durkheim's idea of the state as 'a special organ responsible for elaborating certain representations which are valid for the collectivity' and are 'distinguished from other collective representations by their higher degree of consciousness and reflection'.[18] Such conceptions, however, persistently disregard one of the principal elements in political life, namely, the struggles that have taken place, and still take place, precisely over the 'legitimacy' of any established system of political power, and over the exclusion of some members of society – frequently a majority of the population – from any effective participation in the determination of collective goals (which are often in fact, as Marx observed, representations of an illusory, spurious 'general interest'), whether by a restriction of political rights (for example, the right to vote), by coercion or by ideological manipulation.

The questions posed by these theories of political power and the state – concerning the development of the state, its relation to other spheres of social activity, its repressive or representative character – themselves suggest criteria for defining different types of political system. One issue – that of the origins of the state – seems to me, however, unrewarding to pursue. Present-day stateless societies are not necessarily representative of all, or even most, of the earliest human communities, many of which may have had from the beginning some differentiation of political functions based upon age or gender; and in any event enquiry into such questions remains largely speculative. Moreover, stateless societies are either small tribal societies, or small communities within a larger political system, and their political arrangements do not tell us a great deal that is relevant to the great majority of human societies. Only in one respect is a consideration of their characteristics illuminating, in emphasizing the fact that the state is not the only means by which the cohesion of a society is assured, and so giving some support to those liberal pluralist theories which treat the state as one association among others, and not always the most important. As MacIver argued:

> under the most absolute state, use and wont, custom and tradition, social authority underived from the state but instead the very ground of political power, were far more effective forces in the organization of communal life.... The organization of the state is not all social organization; the ends for which the state stands are not all the ends which humanity seeks; and quite obviously, the ways in which the state pursues its objects are only some of the ways in which within society men strive for the objects of their desire.[19]

But of course the pluralist view does not depend for its plausibility upon, nor has it usually been related to, the evidence from stateless societies.

A far more significant question than that of origins – one which is also more amenable to historical enquiry – is that concerning the actual development and organization of the state in its diverse manifestations. Here, the items of contention in the theories of the state appear as features which can be used to characterize each particular state; for we need to consider in every instance the extent to which the state is independent of other social spheres, or on the contrary is subordinate to 'constellations of interest' which themselves have to be specified, and further, the degree to which the state is a repressive agency which dominates society (and what the sources of that domination are), or is rather the executive body of society as a whole. These criteria, however, are still inadequate for constructing a satisfactory typology of political systems. First, it is necessary to take account of changes in the scale of societies, whether brought about by a growth of population or by political and military means, as in the creation of nation states out of numerous smaller units in Western Europe between the sixteenth and nineteenth centuries (see Chapter 5) or in the process of imperialist conquest and expansion. Secondly, we must pay attention to the extension of the activities of the state itself, which results not only from the increasing scale of societies, but also from many other influences that encourage state intervention; and to take a specific example, those influences which effected the transition from a 'night-watchman state' to a 'welfare state'.

The criteria mentioned above have often been employed, as was noted at the beginning of this chapter, in the construction of very broad evolutionary schemes, but these have been increasingly criticized – in Marxist thought as elsewhere – for their excessively abstract depiction of the 'stages of development' which seem to fit very loosely the actual changes in political systems in different regions of the world and in determinate historical periods. It now seems more fruitful to many political scientists and sociologists to concentrate their analysis upon the political structure and processes of change within fairly well defined types of political system – tribal societies, city-states, bureaucratic empires and other imperial regimes, absolutist states, socialist or capitalist industrial states, and so on – without attempting to locate them in some all-embracing historical scheme. Of course, such studies still need some general concepts, which may be relevant in analyzing any political system, and they may also arrive at conclusions about the relative importance of diverse elements – property ownership, social classes, political elites however constituted, military power, and myth and ideology as means of legitimating authority – which affect its character in greater or lesser degree. Thus, a number of studies by anthropologists (Gluckman, 1965; Balandier, 1970; Godelier, 1977, part IV) have emphasized the influence of myth and ideology in tribal societies, and have indicated similarities in their function in other types of society, including the modern industrial societies. Other more general studies, largely critical of Marxism, have distinguished several sources of power – the economy, the polity, ideology and military force – in the constitution, maintenance and change of political systems (Mann, 1986). Skocpol (1979), in a study of three revolutions, concludes that although 'questions of state power *have* been basic in social-revolutionary transformations ... state power cannot be understood only as an instrument of class domination, nor can changes in state structure be explained primarily in terms of class conflicts' (p. 284); while Hall (1985), in contrasting agrarian civilizations with industrial societies is mainly concerned, as was Max Weber, with the 'rise of the West' as a modernizing, progressive force, and with its possible decline as industrialization spreads throughout the world. Within such broad frameworks as these it also seems likely, however, that political sociologists will in future give more attention to the distinctive cultural traditions and historical experiences, and the specific conditions and problems, which a particular state, or group of states, confronts. A good example of what is involved in such studies is provided by a critical review of theories concerning Latin American political development (Graciarena and Franco, 1978), in which the authors note the central importance of the conception of the 'developmentalist' state in its various forms, and the insistence by many social scientists in recent years upon the need to study the course of history with the aid of categories which are 'historically relevant' to Latin America.

This example also illumines another important feature in the construction of a typology of political systems. At the beginning of this chapter I noted how the distinctions made between political systems often emerged from current political conflicts and preoccupations, and this feature is very much in evidence in the political sociology of recent decades. It is not the case that we can or do simply distinguish, in a completely neutral way, some major historical types of political system, even in the non-evolutionist manner that I have suggested; for on one side, what is seen to be significant in the past is influenced by current concerns, and on the other side these concerns have, in any case, a very great practical importance and are bound to engage much of the attention of political thinkers. There is nothing surprising, therefore, in the fact that new conceptions should have been formulated – of the 'developmentalist' state, the 'interventionist' state, the particular forms of the state in 'industrial' or 'post-industrial' societies – or that political development in the twentieth century and its antecedents in the nineteenth century should have been reinterpreted in terms of democracy and totalitarianism, and of the rise of the nation state as well as the growth of the socialist movement. These issues, in the context of diverse typologies of political systems and the state, will be considered further in the following chapters.

4   Political Change and Conflict

Political change of some kind goes on continuously in every society, in response to a variety of changing internal and external conditions, which include the relation to nature and to other societies, the interaction of groups within each society, and the unceasing circulation of personnel through the disappearance of older generations and the rise of new ones. Depending upon the type of society concerned, more or less significant political changes may result from the introduction of a new technology; from trade or warfare; from a palace coup, a change of dynasty, the accession of a competent or incompetent monarch, or the emergence of an exceptionally talented political leader; from cultural and intellectual movements, from the rise and fall of particular social groups, among them classes, religious and cultural groups, and elites which represent distinct social interests.

These diverse influences have received unequal attention from social scientists, and the particular significance accorded to any one of them has varied. Economic changes have been generally recognized as being very important, but their influence has been conceived in diverse ways. Marx's theory of the major historical transitions from one type of society to another discovers their prime cause in changes in the 'mode of production of material life', which result from the development of the forces of production and bring about a more or less rapid transformation of the 'entire immense superstructure' in a period of social revolution. For several decades, however, there has been a great deal of controversy among Marxist scholars about the theory of modes of production, the base/superstructure model, and the relation between the structural characteristics (including contradictions) of a particular form of society and the conscious actions of social classes and other groups, which has led to quite extensive revisions of Marxist theory, and in some cases to a critical reassessment of fundamental concepts in the theory (Bottomore, 1992b).

An alternative theory, still concerned with major transitions in relation to economic changes, is that which conceives the turning-point in social life as being the emergence and development of industrial soc. ᵗy, in which the growth of modern science and technology plays a crucial role (Aron, 1967); and a further extension of the theory, in more recent discussions of 'post-industrial' society, affirms even more strongly the overwhelming importance in the economy and society of the production of theoretical knowledge.[1] What is common to all these conceptions is the idea that economic development, based upon the growth of science – and even some kind of 'technological imperative' – has a pervasive and fundamental influence upon the whole of social and cultural life, and hence determines to a large extent the nature of political struggles, bringing into prominence new social groups, changing the balance of power between nations, and promoting an ever-growing intervention of the state in the economy.

The theories considered so far deal for the most part with major changes in the form of society, but it is evident that there are more continuous, relatively small-scale changes which affect political life. Thus Pirenne (1914), in his study of the development of capitalism, distinguished its various stages in terms of the principal directions of economic activity and the social groups which took the leading role at each stage; and many historical studies of elites have similarly concentrated attention upon the rise and decline of particular economic groups.[2] So far as I know, however, there have not been any comprehensive studies of the rise and fall of various economic groups in more recent times, nor has there been an attempt to provide, on a broad scale, an economic interpretation of political events in the twentieth century, although there are of course many elements of such an interpretation in recent Marxist debates about modes of production, in the analyses of development and underdevelopment, and in the theories of industrial and post-industrial societies. What is clear, at all events, from the available studies of both earlier and more recent periods, is that economic and technological changes accomplish their political effects through the actions of specific social groups which are formed as a result of these changes. Hence we shall need to examine, in due course, the formation and development of social classes, diverse elites (economic, political and cultural), generational and other groups.

By comparison with the attention devoted to the economic influences upon politics there has been relatively little sociological analysis of the political consequences of war, in spite of its manifest importance in the development of societies. Some of the early sociologists regarded warfare as the means by which the first great step in social development – the expansion of human societies – was accomplished,[3] while others have seen it as the principal factor in the formation of the state itself.[4]

It is evident that warfare has continued to be an important factor in these processes of expansion and consolidation of state power. In all periods of recorded history the political order in particular regions, or in the world as a whole, has been very largely a product of conquest and the establishment of empires, armed struggles for national independence, and conflicts among dynasties, empires or nation states. War has frequently brought new nations into existence, as did the American War of Independence and many other wars fought for national liberation or unification, both earlier and later, or has destroyed old political systems; and defeat in war has sometimes created conditions favourable to a successful internal revolution, as in Russia in 1917, or to the emergence of independent nations from an imperial system, as in the Habsburg Empire in 1918. This close association between war and revolution will need to be examined more fully at a later stage. On the other hand, conquest and the growth of empires have created larger political units, and even after their dissolution may leave behind as a more enduring residue some elements of a distinctive civilization, in such forms as Roman law or British parliamentary democracy.

With the growth of societies war has tended to increase in scale and intensity, reaching a peak in certain periods. One such period was the seventeenth century in Western Europe, an age characterized by the early development of capitalism and of nation states, and by religious wars; another is the twentieth century, during which wars of long duration and great destructiveness have been fought on a global scale. The warfare of the twentieth century has some distinctive features: first, it involves 'total war', in the sense that whole populations and economies are mobilized for the prosecution of war; and secondly, it is marked by extremely rapid technological advances in the weapons employed. As a result, it may be argued, a certain 'militarization' of society has taken place in the major industrial nations. Readiness for war, as well as the actual waging of war, becomes a principal political concern, military leaders acquire a more prominent place in the political system, and the economy is geared increasingly to military needs, giving rise to what has been called the 'military-industrial complex' as one of the main centres of power and of economic growth. A UNESCO report of 1971 indicated that in 1967 the nations of the world as a whole spent 7.2 per cent of their gross national product (GNP) on military needs, compared with 5 per cent on education and 2.5 per cent on health. Since then, however, there has been some decrease in military spending; in the early 1980s it was estimated at 4.5 per cent of global GNP, lower than public expenditure on education though still higher than that on health services (Sivard, 1982), and in the 1990s, with the ending of the cold war, it may be expected to decline more rapidly.

The preceding discussion is not intended to suggest that war is a wholly autonomous factor in political life. Clearly, war is an instrument of policy, and the different forms which it takes are influenced by social and cultural conditions. The various theories of war have attempted to explain its incidence, scale and intensity in terms of such influences;[5] and in the case of modern war Marxist thinkers have distinguished between wars arising from imperialist rivalries, those resulting from conflicts between socialist and capitalist countries, and anti-colonial wars of liberation, while other social theorists have emphasized the strength of nationalism and the rivalry between nation states, pointing out that national interests may give rise to military confrontations and the use of armed force even among 'socialist' countries, as was the case in Hungary (1956) and Czechoslovakia (1968), and briefly in the relations between the Soviet Union and China. But however the causes may be conceived, it remains that war itself is one of the major forms of political conflict, and that war has important and far-reaching political consequences.

Even more than in the case of war, political sociologists have tended to neglect the more subtle, less blatant influences which affect political change. So far as the succession of generations is concerned, the major analysis remains that of Karl Mannheim (1928), who argued that a generation has 'a certain structural resemblance' to class position:

> the fact of belonging to the same class, and that of belonging to the same generation or age group, have this in common, that both endow the individuals sharing in them with a common location in the social and historical process, and thereby limit them to a specific range of potential experience, predisposing them for a certain characteristic mode of thought and experience, and a characteristic type of historically relevant action.

Mannheim recognized that the prominence given to generational differences, and the likelihood that organized generational groups would be formed, depended upon many other social conditions. At various times in the past a 'younger generation' has vigorously asserted its claims to cultural and political leadership; a notable recent example, which helped to reawaken the interest of social scientists in the problem of generations, being the youth movements (especially the student movement) and 'youth culture' of the 1960s, which had, for a time at least, and perhaps in a more enduring way, a considerable impact upon cultural and political life in the industrial countries. Such a phenomenon may be explained in various ways, but one factor of acknowledged importance is certainly the rapidity of economic and social change, which tends to separate more sharply the experience, expectations and outlook of older and younger generations, as Mead (1970) argued in a study in which she likened the 'dissident young' to pioneers who are exploring a new time rather than a new country.

Mannheim's comparison between belonging to a generation and belonging to a class also provides a model for the analysis of other important 'common locations', such as those constituted by ethnicity or gender. The social movements based upon the latter affiliations, which were discussed in Chapter 2, have assumed much greater political importance during the past few decades, and their development, like that of youth movements, needs to be examined in relation to wider social changes. Equally, however, they embody and express distinct cultural orientations, and like all 'common locations in the social and historical process' they have to be seen also in the context of cultural movements. The framework in which political scientists usually consider these aspects of politics, employing the notions of 'political culture' and 'political socialization', is too narrow to encompass all the relevant phenomena, and it is more fruitful, I think, to start from the conception of 'cultural reproduction' (Bourdieu and Passeron, 1977), which has the great merit of emphasizing that the ideas and values shaping political action are not necessarily expressed in an overtly political form, and of relating such ideas and values to the whole social structure.

Reproduction, as the term is used by Marxist thinkers, refers to the process whereby a given form of society, or social formation, maintains itself – that is to say, is continually re-created – in that form. In this process a particular economic system or mode of production, a political system or form of the state, and cultural norms, although they undergo a partly autonomous development, are nevertheless connected with each other in such a way as to reproduce a total society. From this standpoint, the cultural system, even in its most 'unpolitical' manifestations, is seen as an important element in political domination. Thus Bourdieu and Passeron analyze the role of what they call 'symbolic violence' in maintaining a system of power, and investigate the subtle and complex dependence of the educational system on class relations, in spite of its relative autonomy; while Offe (1976) has examined and criticized the 'achievement principle' as a pervasive ideology which legitimates inequality in a capitalist society.

Evidently, cultural reproduction in this sense is not an automatic or uncontested process. Counter-cultures may and do emerge and establish themselves;[6] 'legitimation crises' may occur in which the prevailing cultural norms lose their persuasive force and political domination is endangered (Habermas, 1976). What the theory of reproduction brings to light, however, is the dense network of economic, political and cultural ideas and practices in everyday life – especially in modern industrial societies – which constitutes a formidable obstacle to any large-scale radical political change.

This preliminary discussion suggests a number of distinctions which are indispensable for a more profound analysis of the processes of political change and conflict. It is necessary to distinguish between gradual and abrupt, minor and major, peaceful and violent political changes; and so far as is possible to connect these diverse phenomena with their causes or conditions. As I have already noted, some kind of political change goes on at all times, produced by the succession of generations, the rise and fall of dynasties, competition among various social groups, economic and cultural developments, changing external circumstances, and more idiosyncratic factors, which can only be understood fully through detailed historical studies. In the modern democracies such gradual changes are partly institutionalized in the competition among political parties, and in the influence upon government of a variety of social movements and interest groups; and they are expressed, for the most part, in a continually revised and expanded body of legislation.

Political changes of this sort may be gradual and minor but they need not be peaceful. The replacement of a dynasty or other ruling group has frequently been accomplished by political assassinations or other forms of violence, yet without producing any fundamental change in the political system, still less in society as a whole. More generally, however, we have to pose the question whether in certain conditions gradual and minor changes – disregarding the amount of violence they involve – may not be cumulative, and lead eventually to major transformations. One of the principal forms in which this question has been discussed is the long-standing debate in the socialist movement about 'reformist' and 'revolutionary' political strategies. In broad terms, the division has been between those who see an accumulation of reforms and a gradual erosion of bourgeois dominance as leading to a situation in which a relatively easy and peaceful transition to a socialist society will be achieved; and those who regard reforms largely as mere palliatives, value the struggle for reforms mainly for its effect in developing working-class consciousness and organization, and envisage the achievement of socialism as a more abrupt event ensuing from a more or less violent final confrontation between the bourgeoisie and the proletariat. On both sides, however, these views may merge into others which are more starkly contrasted: the idea of a reformist path to socialism may be transformed into a total preoccupation with reforming the existing society and a virtual renunciation of socialism as the ultimate goal; the revolutionary approach may develop into a rejection of every kind of struggle for reforms as being positively inimical to the growth of a revolutionary class consciousness, the adoption of a *politique du pire* and the expectation of a catastrophic breakdown of capitalism from which a band of dedicated revolutionaries will lead the masses into socialism.

There is implicit in this socialist debate, and in the wider discussion of reform and revolution, a specific conception of what constitutes a major change in the political system. For Marxist thinkers this has usually meant the accession to power of a new class, involving the transformation of the whole social system, as in the transition from feudalism to capitalism, or from capitalism to socialism. It is in this sense that Marx distinguished, initially in his 'Contribution to a Critique of Hegel's Philosophy of Right' (1844), between 'a partial, *merely* political revolution which leaves the pillars of the building standing', and a social revolution; thereby changing the whole concept of revolution, as Max Adler (1928) later argued, 'from the merely political idea of the transformation of the state, into the social concept of an economic change in the bases of society'.

Liberal social thinkers, on the other hand, have generally been less inclined to delineate quite so sharply vast historical epochs in which distinct types of political system prevailed, or to assert such a close relation between the political system and the structure of society.[7] For the most part, therefore, they have conceived major political changes as being produced in a more autonomous way, and less abruptly, with the various stages merging into each other; for example, in their accounts of the growth and consolidation of individual liberty, or of the development of modern democracy.

Some problems in the Marxist theory of history, and various new interpretations of it which allow a greater autonomy to political changes – for example, the emergence of the absolutist state – were discussed earlier; and in the present context I would like to focus attention upon two more recent phenomena, and to ask whether or not they can be considered as major changes of political regime. First, are we to regard the welfare state, which fits uneasily, if at all, into a Marxist scheme, as a new type of state, which differs in fundamental respects from the state as it existed in the *laissez-faire* capitalist societies of the nineteenth century? Evidently, diverse interpretations are possible. It may be argued, though I think with difficulty, that there is no important difference between the modern welfare state and the nineteenth-century 'night watchman' state, in so far as it is still an instrument of bourgeois domination; or that the welfare state – involving a high level of government intervention in the economy, the provision of extensive social services and a considerable degree of national economic planning – corresponds with a new stage in the development of capitalism, which may be called 'organized capitalism'; or finally, that the welfare state is a particular stage in a general trend toward collectivism, inspired mainly by the labour movement, and from this aspect can be regarded as a transitional stage on the way to socialism.[8] The two latter accounts, which seem to me much more plausible than the first, both recognize, in their different ways, that the welfare state is a distinct type of political regime, formed in societies which have experienced major changes in their economic systems, social relationships and cultural orientations during the past century.

A second instance of political change which can scarcely be regarded as minor is the rise and fall of the fascist regimes in Europe. There is an immense difference between the political systems of fascism and of liberal democracy, either of which may exist in a capitalist society; and no one can doubt that the history of the world would have been very different if the fascist powers had been victorious in the Second World War. But the distinctiveness of fascism has been variously interpreted. In the 1920s and 1930s some Marxists – and particularly those who adhered to Bolshevik views – conceived fascism as the more or less inevitable form assumed by the rule of the bourgeoisie in the monopolistic phase of capitalist development, and at the same time underestimated the strength of the fascist movements. Such an interpretation now appears at best inadequate, not only because monopoly capitalism (that is, capitalism in which large corporations dominate the economy), so far as it escapes regulation by the interventionist state, seems quite compatible with a liberal democratic regime; but also because the rise of fascism depended upon a number of other factors. Certainly, the fascist movements emerged in conditions of economic crisis and fierce class struggles, but their development was also made possible by the existence of large numbers of *déclassés* and discontented former soldiers and officers who formed the fascist militias, by a rising tide of nationalism, and in the countries where they were successful, by authoritarian traditions of government. Hence, from one aspect the fascist regimes in Europe (and the equally authoritarian, nationalistic and militaristic regime in Japan) can be regarded as the means by which a modernizing 'revolution from above' was effected in societies which had not experienced successful bourgeois democratic revolutions (Moore, 1967). From another aspect such regimes may be seen as an embodiment of tendencies inherent in modern 'mass societies', resulting from the increasing power of the state and the extension of its influence, from the growth of nationalism and international rivalries, and from the struggles among political elites who have acquired, in one way or another, a mass following. This view has taken shape in the theories of totalitarianism as a distinctive type of political system, exemplified in the Stalinist dictatorship as well as in the fascist regimes.[9]

Both the development of the welfare state and the emergence of fascism or, more generally, of totalitarian regimes, are undoubtedly major political changes, which can be defined, in the light of this twentieth-century experience, but also taking into account other historical transformations, as those which bring about a significant reorganization of the apparatus of government, a change in the relations between government and people, and to a considerable extent, a restructuring of other social relationships, including modifications in the hierarchical ordering of various social groups. How, then, are such changes related to the massive changes in the whole structure of society, the passage from one social formation to another, which are the crucial elements in the Marxist theory of history? In certain respects, that theory, notwithstanding its immense value as an intellectual scheme for orienting some important kinds of historical enquiry, seems to me profoundly misleading. Its source, in the thought of Marx himself, was evidently a reflection upon the revolutions of the eighteenth century, and upon the broad features of the transition from feudalism to capitalism. But that transition, in the sharpness of its break with the past, its revolutionary significance for the future, has perhaps no historical parallel, unless it be the neolithic revolution in the early stages of human history. No other historical transformation has quite the same clear-cut and definite character.

More important, although most Marxist thinkers have taken it as a model, it provides no reliable guide to future social transformations. We simply do not have any clear conception of what form a transition from capitalism to socialism would take, above all because there is no convincing historical experience of such a transition. To be sure, there is evident in the modern world a trend toward collectivism, but this can assume, and has assumed, very diverse forms: among them the fascist corporate state; the Stalinist autocracy and the highly regulated society, dominated by a single party, which succeeded it; the 'mixed economy' of the capitalist welfare states, in which some important sectors of the economy are publicly owned, a vast network of publicly financed and administered social services exists, and the national economy is regulated and partly planned by the state, which now employs a substantial and increasing proportion of the active population; and the former Yugoslav system of self-management in an economy which was largely publicly owned. But there has also appeared, in the past decade, a strong reaction against collectivism, in the shape of opposition to what is seen as excessive regulation of social life by public bureaucracies, and this has been translated in some countries (notably in Britain) into policies of privatization of public enterprises and services, with consequences that have themselves given rise to fierce controversy. Thus socialism, as the idea of a future form of society, has had to contend with a strong reassertion of individualism and private enterprise, and of civil and political rights against the possibility of autocratic rule; and a transition to a socialist society now appears a far more complex and uncertain process. In the early 1990s there has been indeed a reverse transition to capitalism in the former communist countries of Eastern Europe, and the issues this process raises will need to be considered more fully later (see Chapter 6).

It is an important question how far political change, which almost always involves some kind of conflict, also tends to be accomplished by violent means. As I indicated earlier, even minor political changes may depend upon the use of force, in *coups d'état* or sporadic revolts. Equally, however, some changes of a major character may be achieved more or less peacefully. Marx's concept of a social revolution – that is, a major transition from one type of society to another – says nothing directly about the use of violence; although Marx, and some later Marxists, undoubtedly thought that in most cases the political revolutions through which such transitions are finally accomplished and the new society securely established would require an armed struggle. The most probable outcome of all class struggles, according to this view, is civil war; and it is the use of the term 'revolution' in this context by many Marxists,[10] and by other radical thinkers, which has given rise to the close association in modern thought between the ideas of revolution and armed conflict.

In fact, it is only too evident that major political changes have very often resulted from violence, not only in revolutions and counter-revolutions, but also in wars of conquest or of national independence. Moreover, in modern times especially, war and revolution have been intimately connected. The Russian Revolution, and the revolutions in Central Europe at the end of the First World War, took place after military defeats; and while in China the revolutionary movement led by the Communist Party was finally victorious in a civil war fought after the defeat of Japan in the Second World War, that victory was nevertheless largely due to the earlier defeat and retreat of the Chinese Nationalist armies in the war with Japan, and to the success of the Communist Party in organizing guerrilla warfare in the Japanese-occupied areas. At the same time, it is also clear that there is not a strict and invariable relation between war, particularly defeat in war, and political revolution. Much depends upon the strength and cohesion of the state and of the dominant class or elites in the defeated nations, and upon the policies of the victorious powers. After the Second World War there were no significant revolutionary movements in the defeated countries; and in Eastern Europe, with the exception of Yugoslavia, the major changes in political regimes did not result from indigenous revolutions but were largely imposed by the Soviet Union.

The consequences of war for political regimes are thus quite diverse. It may be argued, for instance, that the 'total wars' of the twentieth century, because they detach whole populations from their accustomed ways of life, and at the same time impose great sacrifices upon them, give rise to strong reforming movements even in the victorious nations; and that they have in fact contributed significantly to the development of the welfare state.[11] In some other cases, for example in national liberation struggles, armed conflict may lead even more directly to the emergence of strongly reform-oriented or revolutionary movements, and to changes of political regime which go beyond the attainment of national independence.

But some important political changes, as I suggested, have also been achieved by peaceful means. The welfare state, although its development has been influenced by the wars between nations, and accompanied by sporadic violence, is not essentially the product of either war or violent revolution. Similarly, many national independence movements, and notably the Indian National Congress, have attained their ends without any significant use of force. Even the establishment of the fascist regimes in Europe, while it involved the use of violence on a considerable scale, did not result from a massive armed confrontation or civil war. In the postwar period, many social thinkers, reckoning the terrible cost in death and suffering of the wars and civil wars of the first half of the twentieth century, have turned their attention increasingly toward the possibilities and modes of peaceful change.

This reorientation of social thought, in new circumstances, has also influenced Marxist thinkers. Engels (1874), in an essay on authority directed against the anarchists, commented upon violent political revolutions that 'a revolution is certainly the most authoritarian thing there is', but he did not go on to consider whether the authoritarianism of an armed revolutionary struggle might not subsequently become firmly entrenched in the practices of a post-revolutionary government; and he could not foresee that the 'dictatorship of the proletariat' (a phrase which he and Marx occasionally used in order to refer to the political dominance of the working class, conceived as the vast majority of the population, in the initial phase of socialist society) would be transformed into a plain dictatorship and a reign of terror, turned against the people themselves. Some Marxists, among them Rosa Luxemburg and the Austro-Marxists, were early critics of the Soviet dictatorship, but only in recent years was there a widespread and fundamental questioning of the whole idea of dictatorship, and a revaluation of peaceful, democratic forms of political change, especially by those intellectuals and political leaders associated with the Eurocommunist movement.

This new concern, among social thinkers of different persuasions, with the opportunities for peaceful change no doubt results in part from a revulsion against the extreme violence characterizing the first half of the twentieth century, and against the authoritarian political regimes which some kinds of violence have brought into existence, as well as from a deep-seated and pervasive apprehension of the ultimate consequences of violence in the age of nuclear weapons. But there is also, I think, a more positive acceptance of the idea of an increasing rational control over the conditions of social life, which brings with it a recognition of the possibilities which now exist for effecting political changes by rational persuasion and legislation, but without ignoring the fact of substantial political conflict or lapsing into a utopian conception of social harmony. Admittedly, the situation I have just outlined is more apparent in the internal affairs of present-day societies – and even then principally in the Western democracies – than in the relations between nations, in spite of the persistent, and not wholly unsuccessful, attempts to create an effective framework of international law and procedures of negotiation.

Furthermore, none of the considerations I have adduced suggest that political violence will rapidly diminish, still less disappear. Ruling groups have obviously been prepared, in some circumstances, to resist or reverse political changes by military force, whether in Chile or in Czechoslovakia. And on the other side, subordinate groups have no other recourse than armed revolt if they are deprived of other means of exercising political rights; or they may find themselves in a situation where their formal rights can only be made effective in practice by the use or threat of violence. In an earlier chapter I noted that a study of poor people's movements in the US concluded that such influence as they had was derived from mass protests rather than from participation in electoral politics; and a study of the economic progress of black Americans in the late 1970s argued that it was 'under the impetus of the civil rights movement and the ghetto revolts of the sixties, [that] blacks gained access to new employment opportunities in business, government, the media, and high paying jobs in the skilled crafts' (Smith, 1978).

Any account of political conflict, however, which confined itself to these limiting cases of rational persuasion on one side and the use of physical force on the other, would be seriously incomplete. Between these extremes there is a whole range of means which are employed to promote or resist political change: the reproduction of a dominant ideology, which Bourdieu and Passeron (1977) call 'symbolic violence', and the elaboration and diffusion of counter-ideologies; economic coercion of various kinds, exercised on both a national and international scale, by governments, large corporations and international agencies (for example, through economic sanctions against particular countries, through the lending policies of such agencies as the International Monetary Fund, and through the investment policies of banks and multinational corporations); protest movements, more or less peaceful demonstrations, and political strikes. Every historical case of political change or resistance to change has to be analyzed, therefore, in terms of a multiplicity of influences, which take on a specific character and significance in particular countries. But it is equally important, in the world of the late twentieth century, to form a clear conception of how the processes of political change in any one country or group of countries are located in an international network of political forces. Undoubtedly we are living through a period of considerable political instability, in which there is a complex 'crisis of legitimacy' (to use Habermas' expression) not only in the capitalist societies but also in the former communist societies of Eastern Europe, and in many countries of the Third World; but the crisis works itself out through an international system of relationships, and such events as the overthrow of President Allende's government in Chile, or American and Soviet military intervention in various regions of the world in the postwar period, cannot be fully comprehended unless they are seen in the setting of global political conflicts.

This international context is equally important in considering, finally, who are the principal agents of political change. At various points in this book I have referred to such agents – among them nations, dynasties, social classes, elites of diverse kinds, generational, ethnic and cultural groups – and we have now to examine more closely their role in political life and especially the conditions under which one or other of them has a predominant influence. There is, however, a preliminary question to be discussed. In the sociology of the 1960s and 1970s, as I noted in the Introduction, much attention was given, especially by those thinkers who can be regarded broadly as Marxist structuralists, to an analysis of the hidden 'logic of structures', or 'structural causality'. This approach is well illustrated in Godelier's essay on 'Structure and Contradiction in *Capital*' (in Blackburn, 1972, pp. 334–68), and in the debate between Poulantzas and Miliband (pp. 238–62) on the state in capitalist society. Godelier argued that two principal contradictions are formulated by Marx: the first being that between the capitalist class and the working class, the second – the basic contradiction – being that between the development and socialization of the productive forces and the private ownership of the means of production. It is this basic contradiction which determines the fate of capitalism, the breakdown of which, and the transition to a socialist society, are the necessary outcome of a structural contradiction, not the result of human agency. Similarly, Poulantzas in his criticism of Miliband insisted strongly upon the character of the state and social classes as 'objective structures', conceived individuals only as the 'bearers' of 'objective instances', and rejected those alternative conceptions which introduce the purposes of conscious social actors into the analysis. In his reply Miliband raised objections to this 'structural super-determinism', and argued implicitly – though he did not use the expression – for a dialectic of individual (or social actor) and structure, a dialectic which is explored at length in Sartre's *Critique of Dialectical Reason*.

In the following discussion I take the position that there are present in every social system both objective and subjective elements, objective structures and conscious social action; and that any realistic political analysis requires an investigation of these two elements and their interrelations. From this standpoint, the two contradictions in capitalism which Godelier distinguishes are to be regarded as being equally basic and important. The structural contradiction does not produce its effects directly in some mechanical and impersonal fashion, but is the source of a conscious struggle between classes, and this struggle is influenced by numerous other social and cultural factors. 'Structural causality', on this view, is something less than the rigorous determination of a specific effect; instead, it is conceived as the production of conditions and constraints within which diverse, but not unlimited, alternative courses of political action and development are possible.[12]

A schema of this kind is applicable to every type of society, and one particularly interesting question which it suggests is whether there may also be contradictions in socialist society; that is to say, in such societies, claiming to be socialist, as actually existed in Eastern Europe, and could be studied in the world today, not in some imagined future condition of things where complete social harmony would prevail by definition. It was not too difficult in the 1960s and 1970s to discern such contradictions in the East European countries, in the form of conflicts among various social groups, and in particular a conflict – which appeared openly from time to time in strikes, protests or even insurrections, and was only with difficulty contained and repressed – between those who control and direct the overall development of society and those whose lives and work are thus planned and regulated from above.[13] Whether this conflict, analogous to the class struggles in capitalist societies, is related to some structural contradiction which would exist in any form of socialist society is a much larger question which cannot be pursued here.[14]

Our principal concern, in the present context, is to consider how conflicts between social groups develop within the limits of given structural conditions, how such conflicts bring about political change, and what kinds of social group play a major role in this process. In Chapter 1 I emphasized the importance of social classes in the political struggles which take place in modern capitalist societies, and outlined the changes in class structure, as well as the diversity of the political movements and organizations to which classes give rise, in relation to recent politics. The development of the welfare state, and the twentieth-century revolutions and counter-revolutions in Europe, are all manifestations of a continuing class struggle in which the labour movement confronts the representatives of capital. But it is clear, too, that social classes have been one of the fundamental elements in political conflict in many other types of society; that slave rebellions, peasant revolts and the bourgeois revolutions were so many instances of a continuous struggle over the control of the labour process and the appropriation of the products of labour.

Nevertheless, these historical manifestations of class action took many different forms, their effects were diverse, and they were related in various ways to other social movements and groups. Thus in the European feudal societies it was not the conflict between lord and peasant which was decisive in bringing about change (only in the twentieth century has it been possible to organize peasants in effective revolutionary movements), but the emergence and growth in those societies of an alien, incompatible element – the bourgeoisie. At the same time, the rise of this new class, and the transition from feudalism to capitalism which it accomplished in Western Europe, were made possible by other transformations and political or cultural conflicts; by the establishment of centralized, effectively administered nation states, and by the religious struggles from which emerged the Protestant sects and the diffusion of the Protestant ethic, which at the very least contributed to the self-confidence and determination of the bourgeoisie, promoted a climate of opinion favourable to its activities, and perhaps hastened its triumph.[15]

The great complexity of class struggles, of which only the merest sketch has been given in this example, is still not the only matter to be considered in assessing the role of social classes in political change. It should be noted, first, that not every class, in all circumstances, shows the capacity to create those organizations which are essential if it is to engage seriously in political struggles. A prime example of a class which is, in this sense, non-political is the peasantry in Western Europe, which Marx likened to a 'sack of potatoes'; and it is notable that even when peasant revolutionary movements have developed in other parts of the world in the twentieth century, they have almost always been organized and led by urban politicians or urban-based political parties. However, it may also be argued more generally, following Max Weber (1921, part III, chap. 4), that 'a class is not in itself a community', that 'the emergence of societal, or even communal action from a common class situation is by no means a universal phenomenon', and that 'the extent to which "communal action" and possible "societal action" does emerge from the "mass actions" of the members of a class is linked to general cultural conditions'. This is especially relevant to the position of the working class in the modern welfare state, where differentiation within the class, social and geographical mobility, changing relationships with other classes, the new functions of the state and the development of 'citizenship', together with a certain degree of cultural unification, tend to weaken the sense of belonging to a sharply defined class with distinct class interests, and still more the idea of any 'historical mission' to create a new civilization.

Even more important, perhaps, in its effect upon class action is the attachment which individuals have always had to some tribal, ethnic, linguistic or national community, with which they identify their own interests, by contrast and often in conflict with other such communities. This social bond probably reaches its greatest intensity in the modern nation state, and it will be discussed more fully in the next chapter. The proposition that 'the history of all hitherto existing society is the history of class struggles' expresses only a partial truth, and the existence of 'peoples' and 'nations', and the relations between them, constitute, I would argue, a largely independent basis for a political world view and political action, the effect of which is to limit the significance and the practical consequences of class membership.

5   The Formation of New Nations: Nationalism and Development

In the modern world the nation state is the pre-eminent political unit. Evidently, this was not always so. Tribal societies, city states, ancient empires, feudal societies, are all organized on some different principle, their political cohesion maintained by other kinds of bond. The rise of the nation state to this position of eminence is indeed very recent; in Europe a multinational state – the Habsburg monarchy – remained a major power until 1918, while the empires of other European powers, especially Britain and France, denied national independence to peoples in much of the rest of the world until after the Second World War. The membership of the League of Nations from 1919 to 1939 never exceeded 54 countries, whereas some 160 nation states, covering almost the entire globe, are members of the present United Nations, and the numbers are still increasing as new nations arise out of the disintegration of Yugoslavia and the Soviet Union.

The emergence of nation states, initially in Western Europe and the US, depended upon two main conditions: one was the development of modern centralized government, undertaken by the absolute monarchs from the sixteenth to the eighteenth century, while the other was the rise of nationalism, embodying the idea of political self-determination for a social group which inhabits a definite territory, conceives itself as having a distinct ethnic and cultural character, and has embarked upon a struggle to establish popular sovereignty in place of dynastic rule. Hans Kohn (1967), emphasizing this last feature, observes that 'nationalism is inconceivable without the ideas of popular sovereignty preceding – without a complete revision of the position of rulers and ruled, of classes and castes', and goes on to note the importance of the rise of a new class, the third estate:

Where the third estate became powerful in the eighteenth century – as in Great Britain, in France, and in the United States – nationalism found its expression predominantly, but never exclusively, in political and economic changes. Where, on the other hand, the third estate was still weak and only in a budding stage at the beginning of the nineteenth century, as in Germany, Italy, and among the Slavonic peoples, nationalism found its expression predominantly in the cultural field. Among these peoples ... with the growing strength of the third estate, with the political and cultural awakening of the masses, in the course of the nineteenth century, this cultural nationalism soon turned into the desire for the formation of a nation state. (pp. 3–4)

In its beginnings, therefore, modern nationalism can be seen as one aspect of a class movement which found political expression in a general struggle for democracy; manifesting itself most clearly in the American Revolution – interpreted by some scholars as the formation of the 'first new nation' (Lipset, 1967) – and in the French Revolution, which together established the model of a new kind of political system embodying the ideas of 'citizenship' and 'popular sovereignty'. The process of forming a nation state did not, evidently, follow the same course everywhere. In those societies where the third estate was initially weak – and during its subsequent development in the nineteenth century became more clearly divided into distinct classes – the bourgeoisie, already threatened by the labour movement, embraced a more conservative type of nationalism, and the creation of a modern nation state based upon the capitalist mode of production was accomplished in a more authoritarian fashion by what has been called a 'revolution from above' (Moore, 1967).

Marxist theories of nationalism[1] have emphasized very strongly this connection between the rise of the bourgeoisie and the emergence of the nation state. Bauer (1907), for example, argued that:

every new economic order creates new forms of state constitution and new rules for demarcating political structures ... with the development of the capitalist mode of social production and the extension of the national cultural community ... the tendency to national unity on the basis of national education gradually becomes stronger than the particularistic tendency of the disintegration of the old nation, based upon common descent, into increasingly sharply differentiated local groups.

And he concludes his discussion of the concept of the 'nation' by saying:

For me, history no longer reflects the struggles of nations; instead the nation itself appears as the reflection of historical struggles. For the nation is only manifested in the national character, in the nationality of the individual; and the nationality of the individual is only one aspect of his determination by the history of society, by the development of the conditions and techniques of labour.

The Austro-Marxists were also concerned to trace the later development of nationalism, and in particular its transformation into the ideology of imperialism in the latter part of the nineteenth century. Renner (1917) argued that as 'capitalism is now passing from its industrial to its finance-capitalist stage' so the old principle of nationality 'the democratic, nay revolutionary principle of the unity, freedom, and self-determination of the nation, is over and done with', and the dominant national idea is now that of 'national imperialism', promoted by the ruling classes. He also expressed the fear, however, that the very widespread and intense national feeling which the war had revealed might lead in some circumstances to what he called 'social imperialism': the imperialism of a whole people.[2]

The accounts of nationalism given by liberal thinkers, who associate it with the bourgeois struggle for democracy, and by the Austro-Marxists who see it as one feature in the rise and consolidation of the capitalist mode of production, merging at a later stage into imperialism, do not exhaust the various conceptions of the phenomenon. Some thinkers have placed the emphasis rather upon intellectual and cultural influences, or upon the processes of industrialization and modernization. Kedourie (1966), for example, finds the principal source of European nationalism in the philosophy of Kant and Fichte which made self-determination a supreme good, and the incursion of this style of philosophical thought into German (and then European) politics following the breakdown of traditional ways of life and stable communities. This 'doctrine invented in Europe at the beginning of the nineteenth century' was then exported to other parts of the world as a result of colonial expansion, and this – rather than any popular revolt against colonial rule – accounts for the nationalist movements of the twentieth century, led by nationalist intellectuals who are 'marginal' to their own societies. But this analysis concentrates unduly upon the intellectual content of nationalism, while neglecting its social sources, and it attributes to intellectuals an exaggerated importance as leaders of nationalist movements.[3]

The relation between nationalism and industrialization/modernization has been formulated most fully by Gellner,[4] in a model which brings together economic and cultural factors. His main argument is that 'as the wave of industrialisation and modernisation moves outward, it disrupts the previous political units which are generally either small and intimate ... or large but loose and ill-centralised'. The 'two prongs of nationalism', he suggests, 'tend to be a proletariat and an intelligentsia': the former is first uprooted and then gradually incorporated in a new national community; the latter provides new cultural definitions of group membership which are widely diffused with the development of mass literacy and a national educational system which industrialization itself makes necessary.

These recent theories, whether they deal with an intellectual movement – the invention of a new doctrine – or with the social process of industrialization, are obviously concerned mainly with the nationalism of the twentieth century and with what are claimed to be its roots in the social, cultural and political changes which occurred in Western Europe during the nineteenth century. But the development of the idea of a 'nation' and the formation of nation states in Europe began at a much earlier time, and in order to understand the vigour of later nationalist movements in Europe and elsewhere we need to look more closely at that historical process.

Charles Tilly (1975), in his introduction and conclusion to a volume which examines in detail some major aspects of the development of national states in Western Europe, considers the specific conditions in which these states began to emerge from the beginning of the sixteenth century, outlines their distinctive features, and reviews the causes of their development and eventual dominance. The national state, as it took shape in Western Europe, controlled a well-defined, continuous territory; it was relatively centralized; it was clearly differentiated from other organizations; and it reinforced its claims by gradually acquiring a monopoly of the means of physical coercion within its territory.

This new type of state expanded, as Tilly indicates, by means of war, but there were some general conditions which facilitated the absorption of the population of smaller political units; notably the cultural homogeneity of Europe, the existence of a uniform economy based on peasant agriculture and a small, but widespread class of landlords, and an extensive, decentralized but relatively uniform political structure. Among more specific causes Tilly mentions the growth of cities, trade, merchants and manufacturers, and observes that 'Later on a powerful reciprocal relationship between the expansion of capitalism and the growth of state power developed'; a relationship which was noted earlier by Max Weber (see p. 88) and is one of the principal themes in Fernand Braudel's (1972) study of Europe in the sixteenth century. This connection with capitalist development is important in considering why some of the efforts to build nation states succeeded whereas most of them failed; for one essential element in success was the availability of resources which could be extracted from the population and devoted to the construction of a state apparatus and the prosecution of wars. The development of a small number of powerful states was also intimately linked with the growth of a large-scale economic division of labour, and the emergence of what Wallerstein (1974) has called a 'European world-economy'. In addition, however, there were specific political factors which Tilly suggests contributed significantly to success; among them a continuous supply of political entrepreneurs, and strong coalitions between the central power and major segments of the landed elite. It is evident that success in war, which was crucial in building large states, depended both upon the availability of economic resources, and upon an effective political mobilization and use of those resources.

This account of the formation of nation states in Western Europe, and of the development of the sense of nationality as a fundamental social bond, is far more comprehensive and thorough than the rather abstract and historically restricted theories which purport to explain modern nationalism and the emergence of new nations in terms either of a reorientation of European thought, or of some general process of industrialization. We have now to consider, as does Tilly, what light this analysis can throw upon the phenomena of nationalism and the development of nation states at a later time. Here, it is necessary to distinguish between those conditions which may be regarded as universally relevant to the creation of a nation state, and those which are specific to a particular historical period. So far as the latter are concerned it is evident that the movements aiming at national unification or national independence in the nineteenth and twentieth centuries have arisen in circumstances very different from those which prevailed when the first nation states were created. All these movements have had before them as a model the existing nation states, and have been influenced by nationalist ideas already formulated and widely disseminated. The unification of Italy and of Germany in the second half of the nineteenth century was a belated achievement by the bourgeoisie in those countries of a large, efficiently organized modern state, essential for the rapid development of capitalist production, such as already existed in most of Western Europe and in the US. Other nationalist movements in Europe had the character rather of independence movements directed against a dominant empire, such as that of the Habsburgs or of the Russian Tsars; and as Seton-Watson (1964) observed, some of them – for example, those of the Slovaks and the Ukrainians – began as cultural movements resulting from the creation of a standardized literary language. Other nations, such as Turkey, have also arisen on a linguistic basis, while the modern Arabic language and its association with the sacred language of religion is an important element in Arab nationalism.

In the twentieth century, and especially in the period following the Second World War, nationalist movements generally took the form of independence struggles against imperialist rule by European powers, or against less direct types of control which create a situation of dependency. The context in which they arose was that of the capitalist world economy and imperialism; hence there has also been, in many of these movements a substantial socialist influence, and in some countries, notably in China, nationalist movements have culminated in a social revolution. Nevertheless, the forms which nationalism has assumed, and the political regimes that it has brought into existence, are extremely diverse. In Latin America a second wave of nationalism, which may be regarded as a continuation of the national independence struggles against the Spanish and Portuguese empires in the early nineteenth century, has developed vigorously in the present century in opposition to American economic dominance, and has been connected more or less closely with socialist and reforming movements directed against the internal domination of these societies by an upper class composed of landowners, and more recently, of elements of a national bourgeoisie.

But although socialist or liberal-reformist doctrines have had an important influence in some cases – in the Cuban Revolution, in the Popular Unity Government in Chile, and in the Peronist movement in Argentina – it is a conservative nationalism, expressed through military regimes, which has largely prevailed. A similar situation is to be found in other regions of the world. In India, the Congress Party, although it had a socialist wing, was to a large extent a middle-class independence movement; and the partition of India after the ending of British rule created in Pakistan a state dominated by landowners and the military, and in India a liberal democratic regime in which there was a mixture of socialist and capitalist elements. In Africa, some of the nations which have emerged from colonial rule are socialist in diverse styles, but others, created by independence movements in which there was an important populist or socialist strain – as in Ghana – and which aimed to achieve some form of 'African socialism', developed subsequently under military rule. The Arab nations, it is clear, are overwhelmingly nationalist, not socialist, in their orientation, and the ideology which largely prevails, and has been increasing its influence among intellectuals and students as well as in other sections of the population, is that of Islam. The tension between the ideas of nationalism and of socialism, and the great strength of the former, can also be seen in other, somewhat different contexts; in Québec, for example, the rise of the Parti Québécois in the 1960s almost certainly owed more to its nationalism than to the social democratic aspects of its programme.[5]

The nationalist movements and the new nations which made their appearance after the Second World War thus displayed features which distinguish them in some ways from the earlier movements which led to the formation of nation states in Western Europe, because they arose in a very different international context – in a highly developed capitalist world economy, in the aftermath of a division of the world among powerful imperialist nations, and in the midst of political transformations resulting from the growth of the socialist movement. At the same time, however, the formation of these new nations resembled in other important respects the creation of nation states in the eighteenth and nineteenth centuries, and even earlier. In the first place, they were conceived by the peoples concerned as an essential prerequisite to any major development of their societies. This is not simply a matter of economic growth, although that has become increasingly important and perhaps dominant, but of a more general development of a distinctive culture and way of life which would allow the society to take its 'rightful' place as an autonomous, self-determining unit among the other nations of the world.

Secondly, the new states, like their predecessors, were the product of struggles among diverse social groups and classes, and the different forms which their political regimes assumed depended upon the outcome of such struggles. Peasants, landowners, a nascent bourgeoisie, a relatively small industrial working class, intellectuals whose doctrinal allegiances range from a conservative, traditionalist nationalism to Marxism, government officials, political party leaders, and military officers are all potentially capable of influencing the construction of a new state. The most significant divergence from earlier processes of state formation is probably to be found in the active role of organized political parties which can mobilize mass support, or of military officers whose strength lies in their experience of modern technology and administration and their control of the means of physical coercion.

Thirdly, the rulers of new nations, by whatever means they attained power, had to consolidate their central control over the society and reinforce the sense of national identity. And again like their predecessors, as Tilly (1975, p. 633) suggested in a comparison with the earlier state-making efforts in Europe, it was their efforts to 'build their armies, keep taxes coming in, form effective coalitions against their rivals, hold their nominal subordinates and allies in line, and fend off the threat of rebellion by ordinary people' which had as an 'unintended outcome' the growth of political participation. The new regimes, of course, differed widely in the kind of problems they had to confront. They might be faced with tribal, linguistic or religious divisions, which provide bases for alternative centres of power; their country might be poor or rich in natural resources; its geo-political situation vis-á-vis other nations favourable or unfavourable; the differences between classes, and the intensity of class conflict, more or less substantial. These differences influenced success or failure just as they did in earlier state-making attempts, especially through their effect upon economic growth, which not only provides resources for extending the state apparatus and developing national education, but is also a major factor in conferring legitimacy upon the regime.

The most dramatic recent resurgence of nationalism and the creation of new states has followed the collapse of the communist regimes in Eastern Europe. In Yugoslavia a savage war between Serbia and Croatia, and the assertion of independence by other constituent republics has destroyed the federal system. The Soviet Union has disintegrated into separate states, and the so-called Commonwealth of Independent States exists largely on paper as a desperate attempt to maintain some kind of economic and political cooperation. In Czechoslovakia the conflict between Czechs and Slovaks seems most likely to culminate in the formation of two separate states.

The process of development of a new nation may itself intensify nationalist sentiment – as it did in the case of older nation states – and give rise to major international rivalries and conflicts. In this respect, indeed, there is no difference at all between old and new nations, and it would be quite misleading to concentrate attention exclusively upon the nationalism of the newly independent countries. During the twentieth century two world wars have resulted largely from the conflicts among European nations, spreading in the Second World War to encompass the rivalry between the US and Japan; and although that war may also be considered from one aspect as an ideological confrontation between fascism and democracy, the influence of nationalism was still very great. It was a crucial element in the political orientation of Germany, Italy and Japan, while in the Soviet Union nationalism was increasingly emphasized as the war progressed. Such kinds of nationalism, which may be strengthened in some cases by the dominance of a particular religion, are not, in their most intense form, generally conducive to the development of a liberal democratic society, as may be seen from certain current trends in Eastern Europe. In Poland, Catholic education is now obligatory (replacing one dogmatic ideology with another), and in those predominantly Muslim states that emerge from the wreckage of the Soviet Union it is possible that some very illiberal Islamic regimes will develop.

In opposition to nationalism, however, there have been renewed attempts since 1945 to create supranational organizations, not only on a world scale through the establishment of the United Nations and its various agencies, but also on a regional basis. But such organizations have had only limited success in restraining national ambitions and averting conflicts between states. The United Nations has been largely ineffec- tual when faced with a clash of interests between major powers, or even in dealing with more localized conflicts such as that between Israel and the Arab states, where great power interests are also involved. Equally, the various regional organizations which have been created do not exclude the vigorous pursuit of national interests. The European Community (EC), for example, actually came into existence largely through an acute perception of French national interests by Jean Monnet, who was mainly responsible for creating the European Coal and Steel Community – the precursor of the Common Market – as a means of protecting French industry and especially French steel makers from their more efficient German competitors;[6] and it is widely recognized at the present time that national interests continue to play a major part in the debates and decisions of the Community. Even to the extent that regional organizations do succeed in moderating the pursuit of purely national goals, as the EC has done, such organizations may themselves develop into power blocs which transpose international conflicts on to another level, in a manner which recalls the imperialist rivalries of the earlier part of this century.

Nor can it be claimed very convincingly that socialism has been an effective counter-ideology to nationalism, or that the socialist movement has in any substantial way curbed the actions of nation states. Ever since 1914, when the great majority of the leaders of social democratic parties in Europe supported the war effort of their own nation states – under a variety of influences, one of which was undoubtedly the nationalist fervour of the peoples involved – the capacity of the socialist movement to bring about a new kind of political relationship among the peoples of the world has seemed more questionable; and the doubts have multiplied not only as a result of the course taken by the revolution in Russia, culminating in the project of building 'socialism in one country', which eventually led to the identification of socialism with the national interests of the Soviet Union, but also in the light of the actual relations that developed between the communist countries in the postwar period. Conflict erupted between the Soviet Union and China, and inside the East European bloc, and even before the collapse of the communist regimes there were vigorous manifestations of nationalist feeling in those countries which included different national groups within their boundaries, whenever political conditions allowed it to be expressed.

This opposition between socialism and nationalism has been one of the most important general features of political life during the past hundred years. So far, as I have indicated, nationalism has proved to be, in any direct confrontation, a stronger force; and it is undoubtedly the case that the most extensive and devastating conflicts of the twentieth century have been the wars between nations, not the struggles between classes. There is plenty of evidence today that nationalism is becoming even more powerful, in the case of both new and old nations; and even within the latter, where vigorous separatist movements have continued to flourish. At present, many new nation states are being created in Eastern Europe, and alongside this process there is also the development, perhaps, of a new kind of 'European nationalism', about which I shall have more to say in the next chapter.

How then is the continuing, and even increasing, strength of nationalism to be explained? This is a complex question, and one which has been greatly neglected by sociologists. Most Marxist thinkers, beginning with Marx and Engels themselves, have been inclined to relegate nationalism to a position of minor importance by comparison with class struggles; to dismiss it (as did Rosa Luxemburg in her statements on the Polish independence movement)[7] as a refuge of the petty bourgeoisie, which would lose its political significance with the growth of the socialist movement; to connect it particularly with the development of capitalism in its imperialist stage; or, finally, to attribute a limited value to national struggles against imperialism, as an adjunct of the fundamental conflict between the working class and the bourgeoisie. The few Marxists who devoted serious attention to the problem of nationality and nationalism – above all, Otto Bauer and Karl Renner – also approached it from a class standpoint. They saw nationalism as a bourgeois movement, but also as a danger to the working-class movement, which might become tainted by nationalist tendencies. At the same time, however, Bauer and Renner initially took an optimistic view of the outcome of the rivalry between the two movements; the multinational Habsburg Empire, they thought, might be transformed into a socialist federation of nations, in which the concept of a 'nation' would itself change and the principle of nationality would begin to lose some of its importance as a basis for the formation of states.[8] In fact, the Empire was dissolved after the First World War into several new nations, though this was probably due as much to the policies of the victorious nation states as to the strength of indigenous nationalist movements.

But if Marxist thinkers have not, on the whole, contributed very profoundly to the study of nationalism, much the same can be said of other major sociologists. Max Weber was an ardent nationalist whose political sociology was guided by the principle of the 'primacy of the interests of the nation state', which he enunciated vigorously in his inaugural lecture at Freiburg in 1895; but he did not set himself to examine with any thoroughness the grounds of such 'primacy'. As Mommsen (1974, p. 37) observed: 'Weber never envisaged any other world than his own, which was largely characterized by the rivalry of nation states.' Only late in his life did he undertake an analysis of the economic basis of imperialism, and even then he brought together a number of particular observations rather than formulating a specific alternative to the Marxist theory, such as Schumpeter produced at about the same time.[9]

In a rather similar way, though without such a strident expression of nationalist fervour, Émile Durkheim's sociology was guided by a concern with the 'regeneration of France', the overcoming of profound internal divisions, especially between classes, and the re-creation of 'solidarity'.[10] Like Weber, Durkheim was hostile to Marxism, both as a theory of society and as a political doctrine, but he was rather more sympathetic to a reformist kind of socialism, although he seems to have conceived it exclusively in a national context, and he dismissed entirely the idea of working-class internationalism (Lukes, 1973, pp. 320–7). Durkheim took for granted the existence of nation states; indeed he emphasized the role of the state as the 'organ of moral discipline', and the importance of national education as a moral education of the young generation, preparing them for their future tasks in the collective life of the nation. Even more than Weber, he was indifferent to the historical contexts in which nation states had developed, or to the possible consequences of nationalism, imperialism (which he does not mention) and the rivalries between nation states. His two pamphlets written during the First World War (Durkheim, 1915a, 1915b) show a total disregard – astonishing in a sociologist – for the social causes of the war; the first provides a brief diplomatic history of the events leading up to the war, intended to demonstrate German 'guilt', while the second naively analyzes the 'German mentality' as a 'system of ideas ... made for war' arising from Germany's 'will to power'.

The much greater interest which sociologists began to show, during the postwar period, in nationalist movements and the formation of nation states is easily understandable, since it coincided in the first place with an upsurge of nationalism directed specifically against the economic and political dominance of the Western capitalist countries – where the great majority of sociologists live and work – which created an entirely new situation and new problems for those countries. This interest has now received a further stimulus from the events of the past few years in Europe. But as I argued earlier, the various attempts to construct a theory of nationalism have concentrated unduly on the twentieth century, and it has become apparent that a broader historical view needs to be taken if we are to develop an adequate scheme of explanation.

Without attempting here to formulate such a scheme in any comprehensive way I propose to consider some of the important elements which would enter into it. In the first place, there are universal factors which contribute powerfully, in almost all cases, though in different measure (see Brubaker, 1992), to the formation of a sense of nationality: common descent (that is, the idea of belonging to a distinctive 'people'), the occupation of a definite territory, a common language, and more broadly a common culture. These constitute the basis upon which the very possibility of a nation state rests. However, they also play an important part in other types of political system – that of a tribe or a city-state – so that it is necessary, secondly, to enquire into the more specific conditions in which nation states emerge. And on the other side, there are political systems (those of empires or of the European feudal societies) in which these factors are less important than allegiance or subordination to a particular ruler or ruling group. Hence it seems right to argue, as does Kohn (1967, pp. 99–100), that nationalism and the formation of nation states depend upon the development of popular sovereignty; that historically, in Western Europe and subsequently in other parts of the world, they emerged in opposition to the existing political arrangements of empires or feudal societies, as aspects of a broad democratic movement.

This is not to say, however, that popular sovereignty *requires* a nation state. Tilly (1975) poses the important question of why political development in Western Europe took the course it did, when other options were still open; and as we have seen, he singles out a number of specific circumstances which, in that time and place, favoured the creation of nation states. Once formed, this new type of state flourished, I would argue, for two closely connected reasons. First, it provided a most favourable environment for the development of capitalism – a stable, well-organized political system, with a rational and effectively administered body of law, especially in so far as it related to property and contracts. The growth and consolidation of the nation state is intimately connected, in all its phases, with the rise to power of the bourgeoisie. As Max Weber (1923, p. 249) argued:

> Out of this alliance of the state with capital, dictated by necessity, arose the national citizen class, the bourgeoisie in the modern sense of the word. Hence it is the closed national state which afforded to capitalism its chance for development – and as long as the national state does not give place to a world empire capitalism also will endure.

Secondly, and in large measure because of its association with the development of capitalism, the nation state has been extremely successful, in terms of increasing both wealth and power; its success being demonstrated by the ability of the nations of Western Europe and the US, during the nineteenth century and the first part of the twentieth century to establish their sway over the rest of the world.

Hence, there is little that is surprising, in my view, in the fact that when movements for popular sovereignty and democracy began to develop on a large scale among colonial and dependent peoples, in the course of the twentieth century, they should have taken as their political model the established nation states, and have become strongly infused with nationalism. After the achievement of political independence this nationalist fervour does not necessarily abate, and may even increase; not only because, in many cases, the new nations remain economically dependent within the capitalist world economy, but also because their own development is conceived as a national task, closely bound up with the policies of an efficient, interventionist state. This last factor, however, is not only relevant to the experiences of the new nations. Everywhere in the present-day world the strength of nationalism seems to be intimately connected with the increasing power of the state as it assumes ever greater responsibility for the stability of the economy and for economic growth. But this, as I have indicated, does not in all cases make for the construction of a more liberal society.

The greater attention given by sociologists, in recent years, to nationalism and the nation state, has been accompanied, it is often said, by a more critical attitude towards these phenomena. Anthony Smith (1971, pp. 5–9), in his general study of the subject, observes that 'The prevailing image of nationalism in the West today is mainly negative', and he continues by saying that this negative evaluation 'contrasts with the favourable attitude of nineteenth century liberals and radicals, and later conservatives, towards the doctrine of national self-determination'. Much of the criticism, however, is directed against the nationalism of the developing countries – against Arab, African or Latin American nationalism, for example – which challenges in various ways the dominance of the industrial capitalist nations; yet it is evident that nationalism is just as strong in the latter countries, though for good historical reasons (they are long established, accepted nation states) it may be less vehemently expressed. Furthermore, the national rivalries between the industrial countries – in the recent past between the Soviet Union and the US , and at present between the three centres of economic power represented by Japan, the European Community and the US – are potentially more dangerous to the wellbeing, or even the survival, of humanity. From this standpoint it may be doubted whether the present image of nationalism is quite so unfavourable as has been claimed.

The present international system of nation states, or blocs of nation states, in each of which nationalism is a powerful force, is inherently likely to produce serious conflicts. These possibilities, and from time to time actualities, of conflict may be observed in many different spheres: in the strains which arise from the redistribution of economic resources between industrial and developing countries, and from the scarcity of some natural resources, which will become more acute as industrialization proceeds throughout the world; in the difficulties of controlling the spread of nuclear weapons; in the more directly political struggles for power and prestige in some regions of the world (for example, in the Middle East and among Latin American countries), and until recently between two nuclear superpowers. The bleak prospect disclosed by this view of present and potential conflict situations is not relieved by the existence of any significant social movement which is clearly capable of diminishing the appeal of nationalism, or substituting a new and persuasive political ideal for that of the nation state. No form of socialism has yet prevailed in a contest with nationalism, and no other social movement has directed its efforts against nationalism at all on a world scale. In practice, moreover, neither the former communist regimes, nor social democratic governments, succeeded in establishing a new pattern of international relations.

The foregoing account confirms the idea implicit in the theoretical scheme which I sketched earlier: namely, that nationalism is an immensely powerful force, first, because it is sustained by a deep-rooted sense of belonging to a territorial and cultural community, and secondly, because this sense of belonging has become firmly attached to the nation state in a process of political development which is now several centuries old, and has taken on the character of a more or less sacrosanct and unalterable principle of political organization. The more sceptical and critical attitude towards nationalism which appeared to develop in the postwar period, and the fresh attempts to create (even within a limited area) supranational organizations, or at the other end of the spectrum to revive local and regional communities, provided an opportunity to redirect the sense of belonging, at least to some extent, upon political units other than the nation state. But the resurgence of nationalism in Europe and in other parts of the world, in diverse forms, has made this once again a major issue for political analysis, and I shall return to various aspects of it in the next chapter.

6 Global Politics in the Twentieth Century

Frequently, in the course of this study, a question has arisen concerning the relation between theory and practice in political life. It is evident – and I have emphasized the fact – that new political ideas have very often been formulated in direct response to the situations confronted by movements, parties and political leaders; and the political thought of the nineteenth and twentieth centuries has been exceptionally fertile in this respect. On the other side, however, we need to consider how such ideas in turn affect political life; how the analyses and interpretations provided by political scientists enter into the struggles between different interest groups, and either help to define more clearly the nature of the conflicting interests or claim to discover ways of reconciling them.

The intermingling of theory and practice is shown in the first place by the fact that the systematic study of politics is far from being confined to institutions of higher learning, even though academic political studies, like the social sciences generally, have undergone a remarkable expansion during the present century. Many important political thinkers have produced their ideas outside the academy while being deeply involved in political struggles. This is notably the case with Marxist thinkers, from Marx to Mao Tse-tung, but it is equally apparent in other influential styles of political thought; that of the Fabians, of Gandhi and other leaders of national independence struggles, of groups of liberal and conservative thinkers, and of those engaged in political action in diverse social movements. In many societies, but more particularly in modern societies, there are numerous different centres of political thought and experience: educational institutions of various types; party organizations (including party schools and research institutes); the mass media; more or less official 'think tanks'; the central offices of trade unions and employers' associations; international agencies; and a considerable number of private associations devoted to political research and education, some of which have grown out of social movements and remain more or less closely connected with them. Among recent movements, the student movement of the 1960s, the women's movement, and various nationalist movements have all produced new political concepts. Some of the most important political texts of the nineteenth and twentieth centuries, which present not only a doctrine but a theory of politics, have originated outside the academy; among them, notably, that most influential of tracts, the *Communist Manifesto*.

The general question which concerns us, then, is the relation between intellectuals and politics.[1] The scope of this relation is, from one aspect, very wide; for as Gramsci (1971, p. 9) observed, 'all men are intellectuals' in the sense that all members of society reflect, in some fashion, upon their social life, including political life, and this is an essential part of their everyday existence. Nevertheless, a distinction should be made – as Gramsci further indicated by adding that 'all men do not have the function of intellectuals in society' – between this everyday level of political observation and reflection, and the more systematic and rigorous elaboration of ideas about society and politics which constitutes the principal activity of more specialized intellectual groups.

In the case of such groups there are, I think, three main types of relation to practical politics. The first is that which arises in the case of a thinker, or a group of thinkers, who formulate the principles of a new political theory, usually within the framework of some broader social theory. Bentham and the utilitarians, Marx and Engels, Pareto and Mosca, the Fabians, the American pragmatists, provide examples of political thinkers – admittedly differing widely in the power and range of their theories – who have influenced political life by giving a new orientation to the actions of classes, elites or other groups in their societies, partly by shaping opinion, partly by a direct involvement in social movements and political parties.

A second kind of relation is to be found in the interpretations of current political situations and trends by thinkers who, while they may not contribute an original theory of politics, nevertheless draw upon extant theories in ways which are especially pertinent in the existing conditions. Some of these thinkers – Trotsky, the Austro-Marxists, Nehru or Mao Tse-tung – have been directly involved in politics as leaders of political movements; others, less clearly affiliated with political organizations – Sartre, the philosophers of the Frankfurt School, modern exponents of liberal-conservative thought such as Popper and Hayek – have exerted a more diffuse influence upon movements of various kinds. Much academic political sociology has had a similar relation to political life. Max Weber's political analyses, mainly directed against Marxist socialism, may be seen as having encouraged in the German middle class, to a certain extent, a liberal political outlook, and much more obviously, strongly nationalist views. In the case of Durkheim,

whose political sociology is less conspicuous, there is apparent nevertheless a strong commitment to republicanism (most explicitly at the time
of the Dreyfus affair) as well as a cautious sympathy with the reformist
wing of the socialist movement and a pronounced hostility to Marxist
ideas of class conflict. Durkheim's sociology as a whole, and in particular
his view of the need for a new moral authority in society, not only
provided general support for the political ideas of the Third Republic
in France, but had a direct influence upon educational policy and the
attempts to create a 'secular morality'. In a more limited way, perhaps,
the sociological studies of political parties and elections, from Michels
onwards, have had some influence upon the manner of conducting
political campaigns, and even upon the prevalent conceptions of
democracy. Schumpeter's theory of democracy, which was discussed in
Chapter 1, shows the influence of elite theories, and has itself influenced
some later political views.

Thirdly, there is a close and continuous relation between the work
of political scientists and the more or less routine conduct of government
and administration. Senior state officials, and to some extent political
leaders, very often receive an education in political history, constitutional law, and administrative practice; political scientists and sociologists (though less frequently than economists) become advisers to
government departments and agencies; sociological research is carried
out to assist in making policy decisions. Indeed, it may be argued, as
Habermas (1970) and others have done, that there is a strong tendency
in the advanced industrial societies for political issues to become transformed into technical problems, thus enhancing the role of social
scientists as 'experts' who can provide technical solutions. But as the critics
also point out, this trend itself has a political character, and may be interpreted as the consequence of the rise to power of a new technical-bureau-
cratic class or elite.[2] In effect, all problems then become 'routine affairs'
of a technical kind – controlling inflation, increasing productivity,
implementing an effective incomes policy, or finding a solution to the
instability of exchange rates – on the basis of a presumed political
consensus which obscures the real existence of dominant and subordinate groups in society and the conflict between them. What is then
proposed as an alternative to this conception is a recognition of the
existence of conflicting interest groups, some of which have a much
greater capacity to pursue their interests successfully, and of the need
for widespread political debate about the allocation of social resources
and benefits among these groups, or in a broad sense, about justice and
the meaning of a 'good society'.

This is not to say that the contributions which social scientists may make to solving particular technical problems, or enlarging the sphere of rational decision making, should be dismissed altogether; only that they have to be seen in the wider context of political contestation and choice. In any conceivable form of society with a developed industrial economy and a wide range of social services there will be a vast array of policy issues which need to be dealt with in as efficient and informed a manner as is possible. It seems very likely, indeed, that an extension of democratic and decentralized planning would lead to an even larger role for the social sciences in the formation of public policies, if one may judge from the expansion and the greater utilization of them which has already occurred in the short period during which the present welfare states have developed.

Of the three types of relation to practical politics which intellectuals generally, and political theorists in particular, may have, the most important for further consideration here is the second – that which consists in the interpretation of current and medium-term political trends, in the light of some general theory or conception of political life. For as I have tried to illustrate above, the third kind of relation – technical and advisory – exists in the context of broader political notions which themselves depend upon such interpretations. On the other hand, the first type of relation is one which has less significance for the present time, when there are no new political theories on the grand scale. Political sociologists, in so far as they are not engaged in mainly descriptive and historical studies, now devote much of their effort either to analyzing methodological problems of the kind which I outlined in the Introduction, or to reappraising and reinterpreting those nineteenth-century theories in which the ideas with which I have been concerned throughout this book – democracy, class, capitalism, socialism, the nation – were originally formulated and diffused.

Marxist theory, in particular, has been subjected to an intense critical scrutiny, from which it has emerged considerably changed. From being a comprehensive *Weltanschauung*, in which there were to be found, according to Gramsci, all the elements that are needed for the construction of a new 'integral civilization', it has come to be regarded by many thinkers as a much more limited and tentative body of thought, which is far from being able to predict, in any detail or with any certainty, the future development of society, or to offer anything but the roughest of guides to political action. In short, it has become pluralistic, and also, since the demise of 'official' Marxism with the collapse of the communist regimes, less widely influential in some respects.

For the most part, however, the various reassessments have not led to a complete rejection of Marxist theory, but to lively controversy about, and substantial revision of, some of its central concepts – those of class, party, ideology, the state, the capitalist mode of production, the transition to socialism – in the course of which Marxism has been greatly influenced by recent work in the social sciences and the philosophy of science. Over the past two decades these revisions had important political consequences, exemplified in the Eurocommunist movement and in the growth of dissident intellectual movements in Eastern Europe. In Chapter 1 I referred to the changing attitude among the leaders of Eurocommunism towards the institutions of Western democracy, and their radical reconsideration of the Leninist model of a revolutionary working-class party, which was elaborated in specific historical circumstances and no longer has any relevance for the politics of socialist parties, particularly in the advanced industrial societies.

One important consequence of this decline, or disappearance, of the old-style communist parties throughout Europe is that the European socialist movement, deeply divided from 1919, when the Third (Communist) International was founded, until the 1980s, is now being reunified. The outcome of this process, which I indicated as a possible development in the first edition of this book, is the pre-eminence in the present-day labour movement of social democratic parties; that is to say, of parties which are themselves coalitions of diverse groups and intellectual tendencies, rather than centralized, monolithic organizations held together by strict discipline and an authoritatively interpreted ideology. This also involves another change, in that socialist politics now increasingly involve many other social groups besides classes, such as those which are active in the ecology movement and the women's movement; as can be seen, for example, in the European Parliament where socialists and their allies in such movements now form an influential majority.

But Marxism and socialism are not the only nineteenth-century political theories which have been presented in a new way during recent decades. The liberal evolutionist theory, framed in terms of the advance of democracy, and of the emergence of a political system based upon what Hobhouse (1911) called 'citizenship', has reappeared in two forms. First, it was reformulated in theories of political development and modernization which were, however, more restricted in their scope in several ways; by confining the notion of development largely to the 'developing countries', and at the same time taking as their model of a 'modern' developed society the existing Western industrial countries, as if these countries had reached the limit of their historical development. Furthermore, they have concentrated their attention largely upon economic growth while neglecting other aspects of development. More recently, however, such theories have been extensively criticized; the concept of development has been broadened again to take account of social and cultural, as well as economic, features; and more attention has been given to development as a world-wide process in which there is a close interrelationship between events in different regions. At the same time there has been a growing recognition of the fact that development may take different courses, and be directed to different ends, in diverse cultural and political contexts. Like Marxism, the theories of development have become more pluralistic and tentative.[3]

The second way in which Hobhouse's work has had a potent, if delayed, influence is through the later elaboration of his notion of 'citizenship'. Hobhouse already adumbrated the idea of a welfare state, which was developed much more fully by Marshall (1950), who defined citizenship as the possession of civil, political and social rights, the last of these being most fully attained in the twentieth-century industrial societies which had embarked upon the construction of comprehensive systems of public provision, including a national health service, more generous and accessible educational facilities, and greatly extended social security. Citizenship in this broad sense embodied, in Marshall's view, a principle of equality which was in conflict with the inequalities engendered by the capitalist economy; and the extension of the rights of citizenship came to be a major theme in the programmes of socialist parties, whereas in the conservative reaction of the 1980s, above all in Britain, social rights in particular were strongly criticized as promoting what was called a 'dependency culture'. But the idea of citizenship also had a wider impact, particularly in Eastern Europe, where the assertion of civil and political rights against the political dictatorships had a central place in the doctrines of the opposition movements. With the collapse of the dictatorships such rights were restored, though their existence in some countries is still insecure, as are many of the social rights established by the previous regimes.

Conservative political thought has also undergone some changes in recent decades, but it has been less fertile, I think, in producing new ideas, though it has engendered much theoretical debate and political controversy. As Mannheim (1927) observed in a well-known essay, conservative thought – as distinct from simple traditionalism – was from the outset a 'counter-movement in conscious opposition to the "progressive movement"'. Initially this oppositional thought was directed against the rationalism of the Enlightenment as it was expressed in the doctrines of the French Revolution and in the practices of the developing capitalist economy; and in Germany especially, it was associated with the Romantic movement.[4] But following the period with which Mannheim was concerned (the first half of the nineteenth century) conservative political thought developed mainly as a defence of capitalism against the rising socialist movement, and so became more sympathetic to rationalist views, especially in the economic sphere. Schumpeter (1942, chaps. 11,13) indeed argued that capitalism provided a most favourable environment for the growth of a rational and critical outlook which might then be turned against the capitalist social system itself. There have been diverse strands in recent conservative thought – among them nationalism (recently revived particularly in populist and neo-fascist movements) and traditionalism (which is directed precisely against rationalism)[5] – but one of the most important is still that which asserts the superiority, in terms of rationality, efficiency and the promotion of individual liberty, of the capitalist economic system over the planned economy of socialism. Thus there is today a reiteration of long-established themes, proclaimed more insistently as a consequence of the postwar extension of socialist planning; opposition to the increasing, more ubiquitous and more centralized power of the state, and to the concomitant growth of public bureaucracy, and on the other side advocacy of decentralization and of what Nisbet (1975, concluding chapter) has called 'a new laissez-faire'. Such *laissez-faire* ideas were put into practice in the 1980s in the US and Britain, with consequences which I shall examine later.

In the preceding discussion I have quite deliberately distinguished various types of political theory in terms of the doctrines which, in a broad sense, have dominated political life in the second half of the twentieth century. For in fact political theories, doctrines or ideologies, and political action are inextricably bound up with each other. As I noted elsewhere, in a study of North American radicalism (Bottomore, 1967, chap. 8), ever since the end of the eighteenth century most of the movements of social criticism have been based upon a theory of society; and on the other side, every major social theory which attempts to provide a new intellectual framework for understanding political life embodies at the same time a particular orientation to the important political issues of the age, whether in the form of Marx's allegiance to the working-class movement, Max Weber's identification with the German bourgeoisie and nationalism, or Durkheim's commitment to the ideas of the Third Republic in France.

Political theories and doctrines are both affected by political conditions and the needs of practical action, just as they influence them in turn; and changes in these conditions are largely responsible not only for the more or less continuous process of reinterpretation of the ideologies of political parties and movements, but also for the more profound revision of theoretical conceptions. We need, therefore, to consider next what have been the most important practical issues, in the closing decades of the twentieth century, which political sociology has to represent in thought and embody in its explanatory or interpretive schemes. The issues can be grouped in three main categories: first, those which have a general significance for the future development of all present-day societies; second, those which arise from the relations between societies; and third, those which are specific to particular types of society.

One important global issue can be summed up in the now widely used expression 'limits to growth'. Heilbroner (1974), examining the human prospect in the mid-1970s referred to an 'erosion of confidence' as characteristic of the mood of the time and attributed it in part to 'a fear that we will be unable to sustain the trend of economic growth for very much longer', and the recognition that we face 'a hitherto unimaginable prospect – a ceiling on industrial production'. This is not simply a matter of becoming uncomfortably aware that the rapid increase of world population[6] and accelerated industrialization pose a serious threat to the environment both by the massive consumption of finite material resources and by the emission of man-made heat and chemicals into the atmosphere; a situation dramatically portrayed in a report by the Club of Rome (Meadows *et al.*, 1972), subsequently much criticized but now taken more seriously again, which concluded that: 'If the present growth trends in world population, industrialization, pollution, food production, and resource depletion continue unchanged, the limits to growth on this planet will be reached some time within the next one hundred years.' It may also be argued that some limits to growth, which Hirsch (1977) called 'social limits', are already operating. In brief, Hirsch's argument is that:

> as the level of average consumption rises, an increasing portion of consumption takes on a social as well as an individual aspect ... the satisfaction that individuals derive from goods and services depends in increasing measure not only on their own consumption but on consumption by others as well.

and 'beyond some point that has long been surpassed in crowded industrial societies, conditions of use tend to deteriorate as use becomes more widespread' (pp. 2–3). Hence the situation we confront is one in which there are somewhat uncertain (in the sense of being not precisely calculable) physical limits to growth, which may be placed in a more or less distant (but not indefinite) future, and social limits to growth already manifest in a deteriorating 'quality of life' and its attendant frustrations, which attract increasing attention from social scientists.

The political implications of this situation can easily be seen. The legitimacy of present-day regimes depends to an overwhelming extent, and has so depended since the end of the Second World War, upon the effective promotion of a high rate of economic growth; and if that rate becomes increasingly difficult to sustain, and tends to decline, as a result of both social and physical limits to growth, what will take its place as a legitimating purpose for governments? In the past three decades we might say that, in Scott Fitzgerald's words, 'life was being refined down to a point', in this case the point of increasing material consumption; or, to put the matter in more political terms, that the industrialized societies, both capitalist and socialist, were developing the kind of narrow and obsessive orientation which Tawney (1921, pp. 106–7) criticized when he wrote that:

> the burden of our civilization is not merely, as many suppose, that the product of industry is ill-distributed, or its conduct tyrannical, or its operation interrupted by embittered disagreements. It is that industry itself has come to hold a position of exclusive predominance among human interests, which no single interest, and least of all the provision of the material means of existence, is fit to occupy.

Postwar economic growth, especially in the past decade of celebration of free enterprise and markets, has generated a more or less universal acquisitiveness, and it is far from evident that in circumstances in which the desires which have been aroused cannot be gratified, or their pursuit breeds disillusionment, socialism, historically grounded in the labour movement, does or can now provide a new direction. For, as Hirsch (1977, pp. 171–2) observes, and as I shall discuss more fully later, the mass organizations of workers – the trade unions – have themselves become more fully assimilated into the capitalist market system and are oriented increasingly to the immediate material interests of their members, rather than to any wider political objectives. What is clear is that if economic growth – which has already slowed down, particularly during the 1980s, in most of the industrial countries – continues to decline, while the claims of governments to legitimacy remain founded primarily upon their ability to promote such growth, then we can anticipate a period of increasing political instability and turbulence.

The second type of political problem that I have indicated, concerning the relations between societies, can be regarded from several aspects. There is, first, the relationship between rich and poor nations, which may be conceived in terms of neo-imperialism and dependency (but in that case imperialism has to be seen in a wider perspective than that which treats it exclusively as a stage in the development of capitalism, important though this latter process is), or in terms of the current pre-occupation with a 'North–South dialogue', which is today more a confrontation than a dialogue.[7] It is evident that however the relationship is conceived it contains many elements of disorder and conflict, and that if there is not a substantial movement, in the medium-term future, towards greater economic equality among the nations of the world, the prospects for peaceful international cooperation will become still more discouraging.

But there is also a more general competition and conflict among nation states, some aspects of which I discussed in Chapter 5, that has proved so far impossible to overcome, or even to moderate substantially. The various regional associations which were formed at various times in Eastern and Western Europe, in Africa, in the Middle East or in Latin America, rested either upon the predominance of one nation state over others in the region, or upon a limited agreement about a framework within which national economic interests could be more effectively pursued; and they all showed themselves largely incapable of controlling the vigorous expression of such interests in periods of crisis. With the collapse of the communist regimes in 1989/90, and the evolution of the European Community towards economic integration and the prospect of eventual political union, this situation has changed in some respects. In the case of the EC, however, there is still resistance to a closer union, notably by Britain, in defence of what are conceived by governments at any particular time to be 'national interests', and even if some form of supranational political organization were eventually achieved this might result, as some critics fear, in the emergence of another power bloc in the international arena, a 'Fortress Europe', closed in particular to the Third World. In Eastern Europe, meanwhile, new nation states are being formed out of the debris of the old system and nationalist feeling is exceptionally strong; and it is an open question whether some of these states will in due course be incorporated in an enlarged EC or perhaps in some still wider, but as yet only vaguely conceived, 'European homeland' (to use Gorbachev's expression).

Within the general array of conflicts arising from the pursuit of national interests there was until recently one predominant conflict, crucial so far as the possibility of nuclear war is concerned, between the US and the Soviet Union, and their respective allies or client states, which affected directly or indirectly all international relationships. But following the changes in Eastern Europe and the virtual ending of the cold war this particular danger has receded for the time being, and as a result a new process of gradual disarmament by the major nuclear powers has begun. The consequences of such a reduction in the level of armaments (and more generally of 'military preparedness') are considerable, for as I noted in the first edition of this book, if there is any generalization about the causes of war which is supported by some empirical evidence, it seems to be that which establishes a connection between an arms race and an increased probability of war (Richardson, 1960).

One discouraging aspect of the relations between nations at the present time is that there is little indication of a decline in nationalist sentiment or in the fervour with which particular national interests are pursued. On the contrary, the economic crisis in the rich countries has led, not surprisingly, to a still greater preoccupation with national economic issues and national development, one aspect of this situation being that aid to the developing countries by the Western nations who are members of the Organization for Economic Cooperation and Development (OECD) has declined as a percentage of their gross national product, while the various protectionist measures which they have taken in recent years have had an adverse effect upon the trade of the developing countries. It is probable that the economic situation in the industrial countries will deteriorate further in the longer term as some of the constraints upon growth which I discussed earlier take effect; and there will then be a much greater likelihood of conflict among the rich nations themselves in the struggle for natural resources, markets and some kind of economic growth, while the poorer developing countries will experience increasing hardship and may reach a point of economic collapse. This analysis points unmistakably to the need for a more deliberate planning and regulation of the global economy, on the basis of new institutions and new policies which would have among their principal aims the control of population growth, a more equitable distribution of wealth and income in the world as a whole, and the implementation of a more sustainable kind of economic development. In short, what is required is a positive advance, however modest at the outset, towards a broadly conceived welfare state on a world scale. But it is all too evident that there does not exist anywhere at the present time an active political movement which would be capable of initiating such a development, and if such a movement came into existence it would encounter immense difficulties. Nor should we overlook some of the dangers – of yet more onerous bureaucratic regulation, and a still greater centralization of political power, both alike inimical to individual liberty – that would attend the construction of a more organized world system. By any reckoning, the path into the future is exceptionally perilous and uncertain for this generation, and political sociology, I fear, can at best illumine it for only a relatively short distance ahead.

Finally, let us consider some of the major political problems within present-day societies. Each society, of course, has to deal with many specific problems arising from its own culture and history,[8] but there are also some general issues to be faced, and the two which seem to me still to be pre-eminent are those which I indicated at the beginning of this book: namely, industrialization and democracy. In low-income developing countries,[9] the achievement of a fairly high rate of economic growth and some expansion of the industrial infrastructure are clearly of great importance, but they depend heavily, as I have argued, upon international conditions with respect to trade and aid. Much the same can be said, concerning the importance of economic development, about those middle- to high-income developing countries which are in the lower ranges of the income scale; but some countries in this category face rather different problems. The oil-rich countries of the Middle East have, certainly, to use their available resources to bring about industrialization, but in many cases their major political problems result from the enormous internal inequalities of wealth, from their autocratic regimes, and from the growing opposition expressed by democratic and radical movements. A similar situation exists in some Latin American countries – for example, in Brazil, Argentina and Chile – where industrialization is well advanced and political life is now dominated by a struggle between classes, the outcome of which will decide whether their regimes remain autocratic, sometimes regressing into military and repressive forms, or become more democratic and eventually social democratic.

In the industrialized countries political problems have a different character, for although, as I have shown, economic growth is still a major objective, this does not involve the kind of social upheaval which accompanies rapid industrialization and the transition from agricultural to industrial production; and it is pursued in a context of other political concerns. So far as the capitalist, or mixed economy, industrial societies are concerned one of the most important political issues can be posed, I think, by asking: what is the future of the welfare state? In all these societies there are contradictory movements, either to limit or to expand the social services; movements which take place in what are still substantially free market economies, but raise the question whether there can be any further development of the welfare state without restricting still more the operation of the market and eventually creating a more socialist type of economy in which public ownership of some major productive resources and financial institutions, and more extensive planning, would have a larger role. In a book devoted to this question Robson (1976) contrasted the welfare state, as a means of providing services to the needy and underprivileged members of the community, with the 'welfare society', in which 'welfare is of unlimited scope', involving conditions of work, income, the character and scope of social services, the quality of the environment, recreational facilities, and the cultivation of the arts, as well as freedom of expression and movement, and the protection of individuals against abuses of power. In his view, it is the failure to develop the social and political attitudes appropriate to a welfare society, which could also be called a democratic socialist society, that is responsible for the limited success in building a welfare state. This failure is well illustrated, I think, by the outlook and policies of trade unions, which have constituted the organized mass basis of all socialist movements, but which now seem to have, at least in some countries, a more tenuous connection with socialism.

In Britain, especially, the political ideas of trade union leaders in recent decades have been very confused; on one side, most of them have continued to proclaim their general support for the Labour Party, and thus for the idea of a socialist society, however vaguely conceived, while on the other side, many of them have accepted in fact the principles of a market economy in the emphasis which they place upon 'free collective bargaining'. What has emerged to some extent, especially in the more commercial climate of the 1980s, is an American-style, non-political, 'business trade unionism'. Britain, however, may be an extreme case, and in some other European countries the relations between the trade unions and the socialist movement have remained much closer. Thus, a study (Korpi, 1978, p. 332) of the unions and politics in Sweden concluded that, with the strengthening of their collective power base the levels of aspiration of wage-earners are likely to increase (in a political sense), 'extending to issues of control over work and production'; while another study (Gallie, 1978, p. 299) brought out

important differences between British and French workers in their
attitudes to the present system of industrial production, with the latter
taking a much more political view:

> The French felt that the existing structure of power was illegitimate,
> and a clear majority would have been prepared to see an extension
> of worker control over management's powers of decision.... In
> contrast, the British workers showed a high level of contentment with
> the existing procedures of decision making.

Thus there are quite wide variations in the political attitudes and
involvement of workers; and the form which these attitudes eventually
take, among both white-collar and blue-collar workers, and in which
they become embodied in trade union policies, will be crucial for the
future development of the existing welfare states.

Those industrial societies which were (and in a few cases still are) col-
lectivist and centrally planned, have had to cope with different problems,
although they too were affected by economic recession, and faced
some of the same difficulties in maintaining economic growth. Their
major problems arose, however, from the development of the democratic
opposition movements, the principal aims of which, in the East European
countries (and also in China), were to create a more open society by
ending the political domination of a single party and restoring basic civil
and political rights, as well as extending the economic reforms that began,
on a significant scale, in the 1970s, in order to decentralize decision
making and satisfy more adequately consumer needs.[10]

What, then, can we conclude about the contribution that political
sociology has made to understanding more clearly the main trends of
political change in the twentieth century, and to influencing the course
of events? The massive, tumultuous and frequently violent changes in
human society that characterize this century have, without question,
formed the substance of major political theories, which at the same time
– because such theories always combine analysis with some ideology or
'vision' of the social world[11] – have directly influenced the shape and
direction that these changes have taken. Within the complex history of
the twentieth century it is possible to discern a number of dominant
tendencies, and distinct periods, various aspects of which have been illu-
minated and made more intelligible by political and sociological thinkers
of diverse schools.

One of these tendencies, perhaps pre-eminent over the century as a
whole, is economic development and the associated rationalization
and modernization of social life, which continues unabated today. The

phenomenon has been well described, in a study of a particular instance of the process, by Peukert (1991, p. 82):

> In an economic sense, modernity is characterized by highly rationalized industrial production, complex technological infrastructure, and a substantial degree of bureaucratized administrative and service activity [with] food production carried out by an increasingly small, but productive, agricultural sector. Socially speaking, its typical features include the division of labour, wage and salary discipline, an urbanized environment, extensive educational opportunities and a demand for skills and training. As far as culture is concerned, media products dominate [and] continuity with traditional aesthetic principles and practices ... is broken.... In intellectual terms, modernity marks the triumph of Western rationality, whether in social planning, the expansion of the sciences or the self-replicating dynamism of technology.

Within this general process of economic development and modernization three main periods can be distinguished. The first, from the end of the nineteenth century to the First World War, was characterized by rapid scientific and technological advance, the growth of large corporations and trusts, as well as large financial institutions which played an increasingly important role in the economy, and growing tension and conflict between the leading European imperialist powers. In the second interwar period, two dominant features were the economic depression of the 1930s in the capitalist countries, and the rapid, forced industrialization of the Soviet Union as a 'socialist', centrally planned economy. At the same time, however, there also began, notably in the US, that 'motorization' of the world which Schumpeter (1939, p. 167) saw as the stimulus for a new expansionist phase in the capitalist economy; and more generally, the first indications of the emergence of a mass production/mass consumption society. The third period, beginning after the Second World War, had distinctive features of its own, above all in Western Europe: a greater degree of government intervention in the economy, particularly in the construction of welfare states; a continuation, and in some countries an extension, of wartime planning; and an expansion of public ownership or of various forms of 'social partnership'. The war itself had an important influence, both on the development of welfare states and on the rapid postwar advance of science and technology; but equally significant factors were the growing strength of European socialist parties and the competition and confrontation between the advanced capitalist countries and the communist countries of Eastern Europe. The postwar changes resulted in a prolonged boom, with exceptionally high rates of growth, from 1950 until the early 1970s, in the capitalist countries (Postan, 1967; Maddison, 1982), and similarly rapid growth in Eastern Europe over the same period. A new phase began, however, in the mid-1970s, which I shall consider later in the light of the current situation.

A second dominant trend in the twentieth century is the gradual extension of democracy, but as I showed in Chapter 1 this was a slow and halting process in the interwar years, with democracy being suppressed in several European countries, by fascist regimes, the Stalinist dictatorship and the dictatorships in Portugal and Spain, while in the colonial territories it either did not exist at all, or in a few cases only in rudimentary forms. After the Second World War, however, there was a more rapid advance: democratic regimes were re-established in Germany and Italy, and from the late 1970s in Portugal and Spain; many colonial territories gained their independence, though they did not always develop subsequently in democratic forms; and at the end of the 1980s the collapse of communist regimes in Eastern Europe was followed by the restoration, or creation, of democratic political systems. At the same time, in much of the Western world there was a growth of social democracy through an extension of the civil, political and social rights of citizens, and their more effective implementation in many cases as a result of the campaigns of civil rights movements. In the last decade of the century, therefore, democracy and what may be called a 'democratic way of life' has become a political principle almost universally subscribed to, though its actual practice still remains very imperfect in large areas of the world.

The third major tendency in twentieth-century politics to be considered here is the growth of the socialist movement, which has been closely related to the progress of democracy. After 1945 democratic socialist parties in a number of West European countries were able, for the first time, to form governments or to become major partners in coalition governments, and thus impart a new direction to economic and social policy making (and this also happened to some extent in other regions of the world, though encountering greater difficulties). This growth has continued, notwithstanding the collapse of communism, interpreted by some short-sighted commentators as the 'death of socialism', but indeed perhaps gaining new strength from that collapse, as I argued earlier; and in the early 1990s not only were there active socialist governments in some countries, but socialists formed the largest, most influential group in the European Parliament. The opposition between capitalism and socialism has thus remained throughout the century a dominant feature of political life, whatever the modifications that have been introduced into the opposing doctrines and policies in response to changes in the economy and society; which were themselves, in part, an outcome of this conflict.

The trends I have identified here clearly occupied a central place in the political thought of Max Weber, of Marxist thinkers such as Bauer and Hilferding, of Schumpeter, and of their numerous followers and successors. This body of thought, comprising the major contribution of social scientists in the twentieth century to the understanding of political life, has three essential elements: an economic sociology, a political sociology and a profound concern with long-term structural changes in society; the last of them being described by several of these thinkers (Weber and Schumpeter among them) as involving an 'economic interpretation of history'. It is in terms of such a paradigm – broadly conceived, and preferred among the diverse methodological orientations that I discussed in the Introduction for its greater fruitfulness and explanatory potential – that I have analyzed political movements, change and conflict throughout this book; and in these final pages I should like to consider briefly the contribution it can make to understanding the present state of the world and its likely evolution in a medium-term future of two or three decades.

No one can doubt that present-day societies have been shaped above all by the massive explosion of human productive powers, in the particular forms that this phenomenon has taken. From this overwhelming fact – signalled, be it remembered, most dramatically by Marx – have sprung a great number of the achievements, problems and conflicts of the late twentieth century: economic growth and the attainment of generally high standards of living, sustained partly by extensive welfare services, in the industrial countries; the rapid growth of world population, due in part to vastly improved medical services; changes in the structure of capitalism towards a more 'organized' form, and in the class system; revisions of the socialist alternative, to some extent as a result of the relative success of 'welfare capitalism'; the North–South divide; the impact of population growth and industrialization on the environment; and the shifting balance of economic power in the world.

It is in terms of these phenomena of continuing change and conflict, of new forms of order and disorder, that current political processes and prospects have to be interpreted. Undoubtedly, the most dramatic events of recent years have been those associated with the disintegration of the communist regimes in Eastern Europe. Their collapse was brought about by opposition movements demanding greater democracy, but also a reconstruction of the economy to achieve higher rates of growth and in particular a vastly improved supply of consumer goods. When the political dictatorships had been overthrown several alternative courses of action were open to the successor regimes. They might have set out to reform the planning system, giving greater independence to public enterprises, establishing more effective accounting and regulation of economic performance, and also enlarging the share of medium- and small-scale private enterprise in production, trade and services; in short, to move gradually towards a system of market socialism or to a mixed economy in which public ownership and planning would still have a substantial place. In the event, however, the groups which came to power in most of these countries determined to restore capitalism as quickly as possible, encouraged in this course by the swarms of 'free-marketeers' who descended upon them, notably from the US, Britain, Germany and the International Monetary Fund. The early consequences have been devastating – a rapid fall in GDP, large-scale unemployment, sharply declining living standards for a large part of the population, the loss of important social rights, and the emergence of extreme inequality – and the mood that prevailed in 1989, of entering joyfully into a brave new world, has given way to disillusionment and hostility. This second collapse has produced a new trade union militancy and a growing influence of re-established or new socialist parties, but it has also engendered in several countries a fervent nationalism, so far most intense in Yugoslavia and the Soviet Union where it has led to military confrontations. This rebirth of nationalism demonstrates, as I noted in Chapter 5, its powerful influence as a primordial social bond in circumstances where an old social order, for economic and political reasons, is disintegrating.

The economic and social instability of Eastern Europe seems likely to be a major political factor over the medium-term future, but it is far from being the only element of instability in the present world system. Thus, nationalism has re-emerged also in Western Europe, in neo-fascist and populist forms, directed frequently against immigrants and potential immigrants (and immigration itself is in part a consequence of the extreme poverty of some Third World countries, and of the economic decline of Eastern Europe). Uncontrolled population growth, the continuing deterioration of the environment, the economic depression in the major capitalist countries, the shift of economic power from the US to Japan and the European Community (and particularly to Germany) and the growing tensions between these three centres, the increasing disparity of wealth between the poorer developing countries and the industrial nations, are all potent sources of social dislocation and instability. Far from having reached the sunny uplands of history, as some have claimed, therefore, human beings will perhaps have to face, even in the present generation, new trials on a bleak and inhospitable mountainside.

The task of political sociology is to define these issues and problems in a rigorous way, to describe and analyze the wider structural and historical context, to enquire into the causes of political events, and to indicate in an imaginative rather than restrictive fashion the possible alternative courses of action. Its practical bearing follows from these aims; for by constructing concepts, forms of argument and criteria of evidence which attain some degree of objectivity and universality, political sociology, to the extent that it is diffused through society, has an effect on ideologies and on political consciousness generally, and so contributes to the shaping of political action. But as I argued earlier, there is in every social scientific theory a component which Schumpeter called 'vision', but which could also be described as the background ideas in a paradigm, that is influential in determining the focus of attention and the choice of central issues for analysis. The account of global politics that I have given here derives in part from such a paradigm, in which I emphasize the importance throughout the twentieth century of the opposition between capitalism and socialism, and more generally between those processes and policies which tend either to increase or to diminish inequality in its diverse forms, within societies and in the world as a whole. The significance of this opposition will be enhanced, I think, if the socialist movements of the future are able to express in a more precise, convincing and spirited way their conceptions of an alternative, viable economy and a new social order on a world scale, as a realistic ideal which can be gradually approached in ever-changing circumstances.

Notes

Introduction

1. See, for example, the discussion in Lukes (1978).
2. See Runciman (1969, chap. 1). This argument has a wider bearing. If it is claimed that a new science of politics was brought into existence by the definition of a field of enquiry concerning the relation between 'politics' and 'society', then it has to be recognized that this occurred over a period of time in a number of scholarly disciplines, so that the new science came to involve not only traditional political thought and sociology, but also jurisprudence, the sociology of law, political economy and political anthropology. Political sociology thus draws upon the methods and results of several disciplines, and is only a convenient descriptive title for a specific domain of investigation and a set of theoretical problems, which could perfectly well be referred to by some other name. See also the comments in my concluding chapter.
3. There is an excellent discussion of Hegel's conception of civil society and its relation to the state in Avineri (1972, especially pp. 141–54).
4. See Mayer (1948) and the comparison between the views of Tocqueville and Marx in Zeitlin (1971, pp. 97–120).
5. For a further discussion of the elite theories see Chapter 3 of this book and Bottomore (1964). See also the study of Mosca by Albertoni (1987).
6. See particularly, for an exposition of this conception, Pierre Bourdieu and Jean-Claude Passeron (1977).
7. There is a useful account of these opposing views in G. H. von Wright (1971), and more recently in Outhwaite (1987).
8. On the 'interpretive' method see Outhwaite (1986); on positivism Giddens' 'Positivism and its Critics' in Bottomore and Nisbet (1978); on structuralism Bottomore and Nisbet (1978); and on scientific realism Bhaskar (1979).
9. On the various Marxist 'schools' see Bottomore (1988, Introduction).
10. These complexities are well conveyed by the papers in Lakatos and Musgrave (1970).
11. Maurice Godelier (1974, Foreword, p. xix). A similar view is expounded in terms of scientific realism by Bhaskar.
12. Godelier, ibid., Foreword, p. xxviii.
13. In the sense proposed by Thomas Kuhn in his Postscript to *The Structure of Scientific Revolutions* (2nd edn., 1970), where a paradigm is said to comprise the symbolic generalizations, models (ranging from the heuristic

to the ontological), values, and exemplary problem solutions, which are shared by a community of specialists – the producers and validators of scientific knowledge in a given field – or by a sub-group of such a community.

1. Democracy and Social Classes

1. This is how Marx formulated the issue in his essay 'On the Jewish Question' (trans. in Bottomore, 1963, pp. 1–40), at a time when he still thought of himself primarily as a participant in the democratic movement, but was becoming aware, as were other thinkers, of the limitations of that movement.

2. In *The Old Regime and the French Revolution*, quoted in Raymond Aron (1965, vol. 1, pp. 186–7). See also the general discussion of this question in Zeitlin (1971, chap. 2).

3. See, for further details of the extension of the suffrage in Western Europe, Stein Rokkan, 'Mass Suffrage, Secret Voting and Political Participation', in *Archives Européennes de Sociologie*, II, 1 (1961, pp. 132–52). In the US manhood suffrage was gradually extended during the nineteenth century, but the right to vote in federal elections was accorded to women only in 1920 (19th Amendment); and many black Americans, especially in the South, as well as some other groups, were prevented from voting by literacy tests and other devices, until the civil rights movements and the resulting Civil Rights Act of 1964 and Voting Rights Act of 1965 brought about substantial reforms.

4. See the essay by Philip Taft and Philip Ross in Graham and Gurr (1969, pp. 281–390).

5. The various sources of this centralizing tendency, and the movements which oppose it, are examined more fully in Chapter 6.

6. This is identical with Mosca's view that the 'organized minority' will always dominate the unorganized majority; and there is no escape from this trap, for if the majority begins to organize it will merely create another organized minority.

7. Effective, that is to say, in achieving national goals, in establishing Germany as a 'great power'.

8. See Mommsen (1974, p. 79). This chapter of Mommsen's book (pp. 72–94) provides a good short account of Weber's conception of democracy. For a critical analysis of this conception see Hirst (1976, pp. 110–23).

9. Barry (1970, p. 14). The book provides a useful critical analysis of the later versions of this type of theory.

10. The name has since virtually disappeared along with much of the obsession.

11. It is analyzed in some detail, and contrasted with the 'economic theory of democracy', in Barry (1970), especially chaps. III and IV where the theories of Almond and Verba, Eckstein, Lipset and Parsons are discussed.
12. For a more extensive discussion see Bottomore (1985, chap. 1).
13. Marx's notion of contradiction, as it is set forth in *Capital* and in the *Grundrisse*, is examined more fully in two essays (which differ somewhat in their approach): Martin Nicolaus (1972), 'The Unknown Marx'; and Maurice Godelier, 'Structure and Contradiction in Capital'. Both essays are reprinted in Blackburn (1972).
14. The idea was formulated by S. M. Lipset in an essay on 'The Changing Class Structure and Contemporary European Politics', in Graubard (1964). During the 1950s there was widespread debate among social scientists about this 'embourgeoisement' of the Western working class and about the 'end of ideology'; for two different analyses of some of the main issues see Goldthorpe *et al.* (1969) and Marcuse (1964).
15. See the discussion of this question, and some related issues, by Mann (1973).
16. See Eduard Bernstein (1899) and the study of Bernstein's views by Gay (1952).
17. See especially the discussion in Rudolf Hilferding's last, unfinished work (1941), *Das historische Problem* (first published, with an introduction, by Benedikt Kautsky in *Zeitschrift für Politik* (New series, vol. 1, 1954, pp. 293–324). Partly translated in Bottomore (1988, pp. 111–20).
18. For Renner's study see Bottomore and Goode (1978, pp. 249–52).
19. See, among others, the writings of Raymond Aron, Daniel Bell and S. M. Lipset. The idea is well expressed in Aron's observation that 'experience in most of the developed countries suggests that semi-peaceful competition is gradually taking the place of the so-called deadly struggle in which one class was supposed to eliminate the other' (1968a, p. 15). I have discussed the diverse interpretations of the changing class structure more fully in two essays, 'In Search of a Proletariat' and 'Class and Politics in Western Europe', reprinted in Bottomore (1975, chaps. 6 and 8).
20. See the illuminating discussion of 'non-egalitarian classlessness' in Ossowski (1963, chap. VII).
21. This kind of analysis is best exemplified in such works as Milton Friedman (1969) and F. A. Hayek (1982). It was also formulated, in a more qualified way, in the course of a critical assessment of socialist policies, by Schumpeter (1942).
22. See the discussion of this issue in Abercrombie and Urry (1983), who also provide a useful general analysis of the social and political situation of the middle classes in the advanced capitalist societies.
23. For general accounts of the Yugoslav experience, set in a wider context, see Blumberg (1968), Broekmeyer (1970) and the later more critical study

by Golubović (1986). With the dismemberment of Yugoslavia in the early 1990s the future of this type of social ownership has become very uncertain.

24. See especially Otto Bauer's (1923) study of the Austrian revolution; and for a general view of the Austro-Marxist position, Bottomore and Goode (1978, Introduction).

2 Social Movements, Parties and Political Action

1. This definition is adapted from the one proposed by Turner and Killian (1972, p. 246). Most general studies of social movements offer similar definitions, though with some differences in emphasis. A valuable earlier study is that by Rudolf Heberle (1951), in which a 'movement' is said to connote 'a commotion, a stirring among the people, an unrest, a collective attempt to reach a visualized goal, especially a change in certain social institutions' (p. 6) and is contrasted with a party or pressure group, for although 'containing among their members certain groups that are formally organized, the movements *as such* are not organized groups' (p. 8).

2. See especially the essay 'Class Consciousness' in *History and Class Consciousness* (1923). On the general subject of class and party see the discussion in Miliband (1977, chap. 5).

3. One good example is the chapter 'A Classification of Social Movements' in Aberle (1966, pp. 315–33), where a social movement is defined in a somewhat different way as 'an organized attempt by a group of human beings to effect change in the face of resistance by other human beings', and is distinguished from purely individual efforts, from crowd action and from technological change (which is directed upon the material world); and such movements are then classified in terms of the *amount* of change (total or partial) and the *locus* of change (in individuals or in some supra-individual system).

4. It would be possible to establish a very elaborate typology of social movements by using the 15 criteria of classification of all social groups which was proposed by Georges Gurvitch (1950, vol. 1, chap. 5).

5. Originally published in 1842 under the title *Socialism and Communism in Present Day France*, the third, greatly expanded edition appeared in 1850.

6. See Lanternari (1963), which surveys messianic movements among tribal peoples, especially in the context of colonial rule, and Cohn (1970).

7. See Hobsbawm (1971) and Wolf (1970), as well as studies of such earlier notable peasant rebellions as the Peasants' War in Germany.

8. See Rudé (1964). The author notes how recent is the serious study of popular movements, and how widely diffused until lately was the

ruling-class view that riots and rebellions are simply the result of 'conspiracy'.

9. Touraine understands here by social movements 'the conflict action of agents of social classes' – though he proceeded subsequently to study other movements – but this is clearly too restrictive. Of course, classes have been a major source of social movements, and the labour movement has remained until now the prime example of a comprehensive, innovative, revolutionary movement; but there are other kinds of social movement, and it does not seem possible to reduce all of them – for example, the women's movement or nationalist movements – to a class movement without serious distortion. On the 'new social movements' since the 1960s, see especially Scott (1990).

10. For a detailed history of the movement, including many documents see Sale (1974).

11. Among the numerous analyses of these events see especially Touraine (1971b) and Willener (1970).

12. On this subject see Lloyd (1971, especially chap. 8) and Janowitz (1964). Some other aspects of the role of the military in politics are examined in later chapters of the present book.

13. Before the nineteenth century parties could be said to exist, if at all, only in an embryonic form, without any permanent organization or stable membership (for example, the Whigs and Tories in the eighteenth-century British House of Commons, or the Jacobins and Girondins in French revolutionary assemblies). For a general account of the development of parties see Duverger (1959).

14. For a discussion of this point, with reference to British politics, see McKenzie (1963, Introduction).

15. On the latter, Nettl (1965, p. 67) observes: 'As these protest parties develop, they increasingly prohibit participation in colonial government, except as a clearly defined prelude to the departure of the colonial power. In all these cases, there is a strong element of inheritance expectation.'

16. There is considerable scope for argument, and has indeed been much argument, about whether the present-day societies of Western Europe and North America can properly be described as post-industrial, post-capitalist or neo-capitalist, and what degree of difference from the nineteenth-century societies in this region of the world is represented by the 'welfare state'. At all events it has to be recognized that these societies exhibit some quite new features.

17. The term was used by W. H. Morris-Jones (1971) to describe a situation in which, especially following a successful movement for national independence, there may be several parties, but one of them has such overwhelming support that its rule is not seriously challenged by any of the others. The history of independent India and of other new nations shows, however, that this situation may not be long-lasting, and that there may

emerge from it either a genuine multi-party system or rule by a single party or military group. See the further discussion in Chapter 5.

18. The point was emphasized by Engels in a letter to F.A. Sorge (2 December 1893), and by Morris Hillquit, a leader of the American socialist party, in his *History of Socialism in the United States* (1910). For a recent discussion of this question see Lipset (1976, especially pp. 36–43).

19. In their first chapter the authors also provide an excellent general analysis of the institutional factors which constrain and limit lower-class protest and rebellion.

3 Types of Political System

1. Braithwaite (1953) calls this the 'natural history' stage of a science, and Nadel (1957) refers to the 'less ambitious' sense of theory in which 'the propositions serve to classify phenomena, to analyze them into relevant units or indicate their interconnections and to define "rules of procedure" and "schemes of interpretation"'.

2. See especially the section edited with an introduction by Eric Hobsbawm under the title *Karl Marx, Pre-Capitalist Economic Formations* (1964).

3. See Krader (1972).

4. For example, by Cohen (1978).

5. In particular, the work of Godelier (1974, 1977).

6. See especially the two studies by Perry Anderson (1974a, 1974b).

7. For example, Poulantzas (1968).

8. On these issues see Krader (1975) and O'Leary (1989); and more particularly on the idea of a distinctive 'Asiatic' or 'Oriental' type of society see Anderson (1974b, pp. 462–549) and Turner (1978, 1991). The debates about Oriental society have been closely related to discussions of the different course of Occidental development and the 'rise of the West', in later studies of industrialization and modernization, much influenced by Max Weber.

9. Perry Anderson (1974b, p. 31) raises this question in connection with the absolutist state and observes that 'There has hitherto been no Marxist theory of the variant social functions of war in different modes of production.' The major discussion of the part played by warfare and conquest in the formation of the state is to be found in the somewhat neglected work by Franz Oppenheimer (1907), but there is now perhaps a growing recognition of the importance of this element in the development of political systems. Thus Charles Tilly (1975, p. 42) in discussing the formation of nation states out of a multitude of smaller political units in Western Europe, observes that 'most of the political units which disappeared perished in war', and concludes that 'War made the state, and the state made war.'

10. See note 8 above.
11. Further distinctions can be made in these terms. For example, India was characterized by Morris-Jones (1971) as having a 'one-dominant-party' system (see note 17 to Chapter 2 above), and although this is no longer the case it represents a state of affairs that existed not infrequently in countries where nationalist movements gained independence and acceded to power.
12. Economic and social administration in modern industrial societies manifestly involves political choices, among diverse policies that might be adopted, and alternative allocations of resources – hence necessarily 'the government of men'. More generally, it may be claimed that there is, and can be, in human societies, no administration of 'things' as such, for every kind of interchange with nature – even in terms of Marx's own conception – occurs within a framework of interpersonal communication and relationships.
13. An exception should be made for the Austro-Marxists, who devoted much attention to the problem of the Soviet dictatorship in relation to democracy, and in the case of Karl Renner emphasized the opportunities for a peaceful transition to socialism by using the existing state apparatus (transformed in its political orientation) to extend public ownership of economic enterprises, and to expand and develop in new directions the welfare services already provided by the bourgeois state. For Renner's views see particularly his essays 'Problems of Marxism', written in 1916, and partly translated in Bottomore and Goode (1978).
14. Mosca's conception of the 'organized minority' also plays an important part in Michels' analysis of the relation between party leaders and members (discussed in Chapter 2) and in other subsequent studies. I have examined the elite theories more fully in Bottomore (1964).
15. In all these respects Weber shared the views of Michels and also of Sombart, although they reached their conclusions largely as a result of a growing disillusionment with the socialist movement, to which at first they had been sympathetic.
16. However there is obviously some affinity between Weber's concept of 'legitimacy', Mosca's 'political formula' and Gramsci's 'hegemony', all of which are intended to draw attention to, and interpret, the non-coercive elements in any system of domination. In recent political sociology these relatively precise concepts have largely been replaced by the vaguer general term 'political socialization', usually without reference to domination or to any theory of the state, although an important exception is to be found in the neo-Marxist conception – which has been widely debated – of 'cultural reproduction', as formulated, for example, in Bourdieu and Passeron (1977).
17. It is so characterized by Steven Lukes in his study of the diverse conceptualizations of political power, which examines in a more compre-

hensive fashion many of the questions briefly discussed here; see Lukes (1978).

18. This conception was expounded in lectures which Durkheim gave in Bordeaux in the 1890s. The text is taken from a manuscript written between 1898 and 1900, and first published in 1950. For further discussion see Bottomore (1984, chap. 6).

19. MacIver (1926). This work is one of the major statements of a pluralist view, which was also expounded in the early writings of H. J. Laski, notably in *Authority in the Modern State* (1919). From a similar standpoint, there is a profound criticism of the opposed conception of the state, especially in its neo-Hegelian version, as the supreme embodiment of the moral unity of society – 'the march of God in the world' – by Hobhouse in his much neglected *The Metaphysical Theory of the State* (1918). This criticism, however, should be read in the light of Shlomo Avineri's recent study (1972, chap. 8), which contends that Hegel's own theory was essentially pluralist.

4 Political Change and Conflict

1. In spite of this common ground there is considerable diversity in the interpretations of 'post-industrial' society, especially with regard to its political consequences; see, for example, Touraine (1971a) and Bell (1973). These debates have also led to some reassessment of Marx's writings on the development of capitalism, particularly in certain passages of the *Grundrisse* (e.g. pp. 592–4), where he seems to envisage the gradual emergence within capitalism of a new kind of society based upon advanced science and technology.

2. For some good examples, see Burke (1974), Dent (1973) and Jaher (1973).

3. For example, Comte and Spencer. On the former, see Raymond Aron (1958), who quotes from the *Cours de Philosophie Positive* (1830–42) Comte's observation that 'there was no other means, in the early stages, to bring about the indispensable expansion of human society ... except the gradual incorporation of civilized populations into one conquering nation'.

4. Especially Oppenheimer (1907), who wrote: 'The State ... is a social institution, forced by a victorious group of men on a defeated group, with the sole purpose of regulating the dominion of the victorious group over the vanquished, and securing itself against revolt from within and attacks from abroad.' See also the discussion on pp. 68–9.

5. The most comprehensive work on the subject is that by Quincy Wright, *A Study of War* (1965); but see also Raymond Aron, *Peace and War: A Theory of International Relations* (1966); Leon Bramson and George W. Goethals (eds), *War: Studies from Psychology, Sociology, Anthropology*

(1978); Alastair Buchan, *War in Modern Society: An Introduction* (1966); and the article 'War, Theory of', in *Encyclopaedia Britannica*, 15th edn., Macropaedia, vol. 19.

6. As I have remarked elsewhere, socialism has been for more than a century the effective counter-culture of capitalism, though it is unclear in the 1990s whether, or in what form, it will continue to play this role.

7. Although Hobhouse (1911), for instance, in his account of the development of political institutions, employed a scheme of classification according to which three major types of society, which succeed each other historically, are characterized by having as their fundamental social bond, kinship, authority and citizenship respectively.

8. As was argued particularly by Hilferding in articles written in the 1920s (see Bottomore, 1981, pp. 14–15), and subsequently by Schumpeter (1942, pp. 221–8) and in other writings (see Bottomore, 1992a). For a more recent discussion of some of these issues see especially Offe (1972, pp. 73–105).

9. One major analysis of these tendencies was made by Arendt (1958). For a later re-examination of such conceptions see Friedrich *et al.* (1969) and Aron (1968b).

10. But not by all; the Austro-Marxists, for example, emphasized very strongly the possibility and the advantages of a peaceful transition to socialism, and defined their own attitude to the use of force in the concept of 'defensive violence' (see Bottomore and Goode, 1978, pp. 38–40).

11. See especially the essay by Titmuss, 'War and Social Policy' in *Essays on the 'Welfare State'* (1958), and also the symposium 'On the Welfare State' in the *European Journal of Sociology*, II, 2 (1961) where Asa Briggs, for example, refers to the 'close association between warfare and welfare'.

12. On this general question of structure and agency see especially Bhaskar (1979), Touraine (1977) and Giddens (1984).

13. See the analysis by Konrád and Szelényi (1979).

14. One example of such a contradiction might be that between civil society and the state, which emerges in the course of attempts to establish their unity; on this subject see the interesting discussion by Kolakowski and Hampshire (1974, pp. 18–35). The concept of 'contradiction' itself – whether it refers to some kind of contradiction in the 'logic of a structure', or to opposed tendencies in 'structural causality' – evidently requires to be elucidated much more fully than has been done by those writers who use the concept.

15. This was at all events the thesis of Max Weber (1904–5), summarized in his later study (1923) where, though also analyzing various other factors in the rise of capitalism, he observed that the development of 'the [Protestant] concept of the calling quickly gave to the modern entrepreneur a fabulously clear conscience and also industrious workers' (p. 269).

5 The Formation of New Nations: Nationalism and Development

1. The most substantial expositions are those by the Austro-Marxists, Otto Bauer and Karl Renner, who had to confront the problems of national sovereignty and nationalism in a particularly acute form in the Habsburg Empire. Bauer's work (1907) has been generally regarded as the most important Marxist study in this field, although it is frequently neglected in the general accounts of nationalism. Thus, in A. D. Smith's (1971) study Bauer and the other Austro-Marxists are barely mentioned. There is, however, a good account of the principal Marxist theories in Brewer (1980), and a useful study of Bauer's writings in particular, in Nimni (1991).

2. For a critical discussion of the Austro-Marxist theory of nationalism and imperialism, see Schumpeter (1919) and Winslow (1948).

3. Brym (1979, chap. 3) notes that military officers have played an important role, particularly in the nationalist regimes that are eventually established; and he shows more generally that there is little evidence for treating either revolutions or national independence struggles as intellectual *coups d'état* (as Lasswell, for example, has done) rather than as broad social movements with which some intellectuals ally themselves.

4. Gellner (1964, chap. 7), and see also his later book, *Nations and Nationalism* (1983).

5. A study of the political attitudes of young people in Québec in the early 1960s, when the independence movement began to develop on a large scale, showed that while socialist ideas were quite widely diffused, no one was a socialist without being a nationalist, and in the group as a whole national consciousness predominated very clearly over class consciousness (Rioux, 1965, pp. 99–108).

6. See Monnet (1978).

7. See the discussion in Nettl (1966, especially pp. 91–4, 845–62). On the views of Marx and Engels see Cummins (1980), and on some later Marxist approaches see Nimni (1991).

8. Later on, as we have seen, Renner modified his ideas somewhat, and expressed his fear that nationalist and imperialist doctrines, in some circumstances, might gain such an ascendancy as to shape the political outlook of a whole people.

9. Max Weber (1921, part 3, chap. 3), and see also the discussion in Mommsen (1974, pp. 41–6). Schumpeter's conception of imperialism is examined in Bottomore (1992a, chap. 4).

10. See the discussion of Durkheim's 'nationalism' and 'patriotism' in Lukes (1973, pp. 41–2, 338).

6 Global Politics in the Twentieth Century

1. In the following discussion I shall consider primarily the influence of political ideas upon political action, not the various ways in which intellectuals become attached to particular movements and parties, or the specific role that they play in them. On the latter subject see Brym (1979).

2. An argument along these lines was presented by Touraine (1971a, 1971b) and in the latter text he wrote:

   Now French society knows once again that its decisions are political choices, even when they rest on the best technical studies and when they take account of the demands of economic coherence. Behind the ideology of rationality, the power of special interests has been laid bare; not so much those of speculators or even private capital as of the massive structures that control production and consumption.

3. One important current of thought in this revision of theories of development has led to the formulation of new conceptions of 'underdevelopment' and 'dependent development' as active historical processes which arise from the complex economic and political relations between 'metropolitan' (advanced capitalist or, more generally, industrial) countries and 'satellite' or 'peripheral' (non-industrial, in many cases previously colonial) countries. For a useful discussion of these issues, see Henry Bernstein (1973) and Larrain (1989). These new conceptions entered prominently into political and scientific debate at an international level in what is called the 'North–South dialogue', and in the UNESCO programme of studies of the 'New International Economic Order' (see note 7 below).

4. At this stage conservative thought had an important formative influence upon sociology, as Robert Nisbet (1978) has shown.

5. See, for example, Oakeshott (1952).

6. See on population growth Myrdal (1968, vol. II, part 6) and particularly Faaland (1982).

7. The North–South relationship was given fresh prominence by the publication of the Brandt Commission Report (1983), but since then very little has been done to implement any of the proposals in that report – or in others – which might bring into existence the much-publicized 'new international economic order'. See also the critical discussion of several international reports on North–South relations by Holm (1985).

8. These include problems of political unity, in the face of divisive tendencies arising from tribal, ethnic, linguistic, or cultural and religious differences, which may be particularly acute in some developing countries, though they are not confined to such countries.

9. I use here the classifications in the World Bank's *World Development Report 1990*, based on data for 1988: *low-income economies* are those which have a GNP per capita of $545 or less; *middle-income economies* have a GNP per capita of more than $545 but less than $6000 (with a further division between lower-middle and upper-middle, set at $2200); and *high-income economies* have a GNP per capita of $6000 or more.

10. The debate about economic reforms in the 1970s and 1980s was expressed mainly in terms of the idea of 'market socialism', on which see Bottomore (1990, chap. 6) and Brus and Laski (1989), but since 1990, with the implementation in Eastern Europe of policies designed to re-establish capitalist market economies, such ideas have suffered a temporary eclipse.

11. This idea was expressed very clearly, with reference to economic thought, by Schumpeter (1946) when he wrote:

> Every comprehensive 'theory' of an economic state of society consists of two complementary but essentially distinct elements. There is, first, the theorist's view about the basic features of that state of society, about what is and what is not important to understand its life at a given time. Let us call this his vision. And there is, secondly, the theorist's technique, an apparatus by which he conceptualizes his vision and which turns the latter into concrete propositions or 'theories'.

Bibliography

Note: in relevant cases the date of publication is followed by the date of the edition or translation used, to which page references are made in the text. Publication details of works by Marx and Engels are not generally given, since there are various easily accessible translations.

Abercrombie, N. and Urry, J., 1983, *Capital, Labour and the Middle Classes* (London: Allen & Unwin).

Aberle, D. F., 1966, *The Peyote Religion Among the Navaho* (Chicago: Aldine Publishing Co.).

Adler, M., 1928, 'The Sociology of Revolution', in Bottomore and Goode, eds, 1978, pp. 136–46.

Albertoni, E. A., 1987, *Mosca and the Theory of Elitism* (Oxford: Blackwell).

Anderson, P., 1974a, *Passages from Antiquity to Feudalism* (London: New Left Books).

Anderson, P., 1974b, *Lineages of the Absolutist State* (London: New Left Books).

Arendt, H., 1958, *The Origins of Totalitarianism* (Cleveland: Meridian Books).

Aron, R., 1958, *War and Industrial Society* (London: Oxford University Press).

Aron, R., 1965, *Main Currents in Sociological Thought* (New York: Basic Books).

Aron, R., 1966, *Peace and War: A Theory of International Relations* (New York: Doubleday).

Aron, R., 1967, *The Industrial Society* (London: Weidenfeld & Nicolson).

Aron, R., 1968a, *Progress and Disillusion* (London: Pall Mall Press).

Aron, R., 1968b, *Democracy and Totalitarianism* (London: Weidenfeld & Nicolson).

Avineri, S., 1968, *The Social and Political Thought of Karl Marx* (Cambridge: Cambridge University Press).

Avineri, S., 1972, *Hegel's Theory of the Modern State* (Cambridge: Cambridge University Press).

Balandier, G., 1970, *Political Anthropology* (London: Allen Lane).

Barry, B., 1970, *Sociologists, Economists and Democracy* (London: Collier-Macmillan).

Bauer, O., 1907, *Die Nationalitätenfrage und die Sozialdemokratie* (Vienna: Wiener Volksbuchhandlung. 2nd enlarged edn, 1924).

Bauer, O., 1923, (1925), *The Austrian Revolution* (New York: Burt Franklin).

Bell, D., 1973, *The Coming of Post-Industrial Society* (New York: Basic Books).

Bernstein, E., 1899 (1961), *Evolutionary Socialism* (New York: Schocken Books).

Bernstein, H. (ed.), 1973, *Underdevelopment and Development* (Harmondsworth: Penguin Books).

Bhaskar, R., 1979, *The Possibility of Naturalism* (Brighton: Harvester).

Blackburn, R. (ed.), 1972, *Ideology in Social Science* (London: Fontana/Collins).

Blumberg, P., 1968, *Industrial Democracy: The Sociology of Participation* (London: Constable).

Bottomore, T. (ed.), 1963, *Karl Marx: Early Writings* (New York: McGraw-Hill).

Bottomore, T., 1964, *Elites and Society* (London: C. A. Watts & Co. New edn forthcoming 1993).

Bottomore, T., 1967, *Critics of Society* (London: Allen & Unwin).

Bottomore, T., 1975, *Sociology as Social Criticism* (London: Allen & Unwin).

Bottomore, T., 1981, Introduction to Rudolf Hilferding, *Finance Capital* (London: Routledge & Kegan Paul).

Bottomore, T., 1984, *Sociology and Socialism* (Brighton: Wheatsheaf).

Bottomore, T., 1985, *Theories of Modern Capitalism* (London: Allen & Unwin).

Bottomore, T., (ed.), 1988 *Interpretations of Marx* (Oxford: Blackwell).

Bottomore, T., 1990, *The Socialist Economy: Theory and Practice* (Hemel Hempstead: Harvester Wheatsheaf).

Bottomore, T. (ed.), 1991, *A Dictionary of Marxist Thought* (2nd edn, Oxford: Blackwell).

Bottomore, T., 1992a, *Between Marginalism and Marxism: The Economic Sociology of J. A. Schumpeter* (Hemel Hempstead: Harvester Wheatsheaf).

Bottomore, T., 1992b, 'Marxism', in *Encyclopaedia of Government and Politics* (London: Routledge).

Bottomore, T. and Goode, P. (eds), 1978, *Austro-Marxism* (Oxford: Oxford University Press).

Bottomore, T. and Nisbet, R., 1978, 'Structuralism', in Bottomore and Nisbet, eds, pp. 557–98.

Bottomore, T. and Nisbet, R. (eds), 1978, *A History of Sociological Analysis* (New York: Basic Books).

Bourdieu, P. and Passeron, J-C., 1977, *Reproduction: In Education, Society and Culture* (London: Sage Publications).

Braithwaite, R. B., 1953, *Scientific Explanation* (London: Cambridge University Press).

Bramson, L. and Goethals, G. W. (eds), 1978, *War: Studies from Psychology, Sociology, Anthropology* (New York: Basic Books).

Brandt Commission, 1983, *Common Crisis, North–South: Cooperation for World Recovery* (London: Pan Books).

Braudel, F., 1972, *The Mediterranean* (London: Collins).

Brewer, A., 1980, *Marxist Theories of Imperialism: A Critical Survey* (London: Routledge & Kegan Paul).

Briggs, A., 1961, 'The Welfare State in Historical Perspective', *European Journal of Sociology*, vol. II, no. 2, pp. 221–58.

Broekmeyer, M. J. (ed.), 1970, *Yugoslav Workers' Self-Management* (Dordrecht: D. Reidel).

Brubaker, R., 1992, *Citizenship and Nationhood in France and Germany* (Cambridge, Mass.: Harvard University Press).

Brus, W. and Laski, K., 1989, *From Marx to the Market: Socialism in Search of an Economic System* (Oxford: Clarendon Press).

Brym, R., 1979, *Intellectuals and Politics* (London: Allen & Unwin).

Buchan, A., 1966, *War in Modern Society: An Introduction* (London: C. A. Watts & Co.).

Burke, P., 1974, *Venice and Amsterdam: A Study of Seventeenth Century Elites* (London: Temple Smith).

Carrillo, S., 1977, *'Eurocommunism' and the State* (London: Lawrence & Wishart).

Cohen, G. A., 1978, *Karl Marx's Theory of History: A Defence* (Oxford: Clarendon Press).

Cohn, N., 1970, *The Pursuit of the Millennium* (2nd enlarged edn, London: Oxford University Press).

Cruse, H. 1967, *The Crisis of the Negro Intellectual* (New York: William Morrow & Co.).

Cummins, I., 1980, *Marx, Engels and National Movements* (London: Croom Helm).

Dent, J., 1973, *Crisis in Finance: Crown, Financiers and Society in Seventeenth Century France* (Newton Abbot, Devon: David & Charles).

Downs, A., 1957, *An Economic Theory of Democracy* (New York: Harper & Brothers).

Durkheim, É., 1893 (1933), *The Division of Labour in Society* (New York: Macmillan).

Durkheim, É., 1915a, 'Qui a voulu la guerre? Les origines de la guerre d'après les documents diplomatiques' (Paris: Colin).

Durkheim, É., 1915b, 'L'Allemagne au-dessus de tout: la mentalité allemande et la guerre' (Paris: Colin).

Duverger, M., 1959, *Political Parties* (2nd edn, London: Methuen).

Engels, F., 1874, 'Authority'.

Faaland, J., (ed.), 1982, *Population and the World Economy in the 21st Century* (Oxford: Blackwell).

Ferguson, A., 1767 (1966), *An Essay on the History of Civil Society* (Edinburgh: Edinburgh University Press).

Friedman, M., 1969, *Capitalism and Freedom* (Chicago: University of Chicago Press).

Friedrich, C. J., Curtis, M. and Benjamin, R. (eds), 1969, *Totalitarianism in Perspective: Three Views* (London: Pall Mall Press).

Gallie, D., 1978, *In Search of the New Working Class* (Cambridge: Cambridge University Press).

Gay, P., 1952, *The Dilemma of Democratic Socialism* (New York: Columbia University Press).

Gellner, E., 1964, *Thought and Change* (London: Weidenfeld & Nicolson).

Gellner, E., 1983, *Nations and Nationalism* (Oxford: Blackwell).

Giddens, A., 1978, 'Positivism and its Critics', in Bottomore and Nisbet, eds, pp. 237–86.

Giddens, A., 1984, *The Constitution of Society* (Oxford: Polity/Blackwell).

Gluckman, M., 1965, *Politics, Law and Ritual in Tribal Society* (Oxford: Blackwell).

Godelier, M., 1972, 'Structure and Contradiction in Capital', in Blackburn, ed., pp. 334–68.

Godelier, M., 1974, *Rationality and Irrationality in Economics* (London: New Left Books).

Godelier, M., 1977, *Perspectives in Marxist Anthropology* (Cambridge: Cambridge University Press).

Goldthorpe, J. H., Lockwood, D., Bechhofer, F. and Platt, J., 1969, *The Affluent Worker in the Class Structure* (Cambridge: Cambridge University Press).

Golubović, Z., 1986, 'Yugoslav society and "socialism"', in Golubović and Stojanović, *The Crisis of the Yugoslav System*. Study no. 14 in the research project 'Crises in Soviet-type systems' (Cologne: Index).

Graciarena, J. and Franco, R., 1978, 'Social Formations and Power Structures in Latin America', *Current Sociology*, vol. 26, no. 1, pp. 1–266.

Graham, H. D. and Gurr, T. R., 1969, *Violence in America: Historical and Comparative Perspectives* (New York: Bantam Books).

Gramsci, A., 1971, *Selections from the Prison Notebooks* (London: Lawrence & Wishart).

Graubard, S. R. (ed.), 1964, *A New Europe?* (Boston: Houghton Mifflin).

Gurvitch, G., 1950, *La vocation actuelle de la sociologie* (Paris: Presses Universitaires de France).

Habermas, J., 1970, *Toward a Rational Society* (Boston: Beacon Press).

Habermas, J., 1976, *Legitimation Crisis* (London: Heinemann).

Hall, J., 1985, *Powers and Liberties: The Causes and Consequences of the Rise of the West* (Oxford: Blackwell).

Harrington, M., 1972. *Socialism* (New York: Saturday Review Press).

Hayek, F. A., 1982, *Law, Legislation and Liberty* (London: Routledge & Kegan Paul).

Heberle, R., 1951, *Social Movements* (New York: Appleton-Century-Croft).

Hegel, G. W. F., 1821 (1942), *Philosophy of Right* (Oxford: Clarendon Press).

Heilbroner, R. L., 1974, *An Inquiry into the Human Prospect* (New York: W. W. Norton & Co.).

Hilferding, R., 1941 (1954), *Das historische Problem*. First published in *Zeitschrift für Politik*, new series, vol. 1, pp. 293–324.

Hillquit, M., 1910 (1971), *A History of Socialism in the United States* (5th edn, New York: Dover Publications).

Hirsch, F., 1977, *Social Limits to Growth* (London: Routledge & Kegan Paul).

Hirst, P. Q., 1976, *Social Evolution and Sociological Categories* (London: Allen & Unwin).

Hobhouse, L. T., 1911, *Social Evolution and Political Theory* (New York: Columbia University Press).

Hobhouse, L. T., 1918, *The Metaphysical Theory of the State* (London: Allen & Unwin).

Hobsbawm, E. J., 1964, Introduction to *Karl Marx, Pre-Capitalist Economic Formations* (London: Lawrence & Wishart).

Hobsbawm, E. J., 1971, *Primitive Rebels* (3rd edn, Manchester: Manchester University Press).

Holm, H-H., 1985, 'Brandt, Palme and Thorsson: a strategy that does not work?', *IDS Bulletin*, vol. 16, no. 4, pp. 23–8 (Institute of Development Studies, University of Sussex).

Huntington, S. P., 1968, *Political Order in Changing Societies* (New Haven: Yale University Press).

Jaher, F. C., 1973, *The Rich, the Well Born, and the Powerful: Elites and Upper Classes in History* (Urbana, Ill.: University of Illinois Press).

Janowitz, M., 1964, *The Role of the Military in the Political Development of New Nations* (Chicago: University of Chicago Press).

Kedourie, E., 1966, *Nationalism* (3rd edn, London: Hutchinson).

King, D., 1987, *The New Right: Politics, Markets and Citizenship* (London: Macmillan).

Kohn, H., 1967, *The Idea of Nationalism* (New York: Collier Books).

Kolakowski, L. and Hampshire, S. (eds), 1974, *The Socialist Idea: A Reappraisal* (London: Weidenfeld & Nicolson).

Konrád, G. and Szelényi, I., 1979, *The Intellectuals on the Road to Class Power* (Brighton: Harvester).

Korpi, W., 1978, *The Working Class in Welfare Capitalism* (London: Routledge & Kegan Paul).

Krader, L. (ed.), 1972, *The Ethnological Notebooks of Karl Marx* (Assen: Van Gorcum & Co.).

Krader, L., 1975, *The Asiatic Mode of Production* (Assen: van Gorcum).

Kuhn, T., 1970, *The Structure of Scientific Revolutions* (2nd enlarged edn, Chicago: Chicago University Press).

Lakatos, I. and Musgrave, A. (eds), 1970, *Criticism and the Growth of Knowledge* (Cambridge: Cambridge University Press).

Lanternari, V., 1963, *The Religions of the Oppressed* (New York: Alfred A. Knopf).

Larrain, J., 1989, *Theories of Development* (Oxford: Polity/Blackwell).

Laski, H. J., 1919, *Authority in the Modern State* (New Haven: Yale University Press).

Laslett, J. and Lipset, S. M. (eds), 1974, *Failure of a Dream? Essays in the History of American Socialism* (Garden City, NY: Anchor/Doubleday).

Lipset, S. M., 1964, 'The Changing Class Structure and Contemporary European Politics', in S. R. Graubard, ed., pp. 337–69.

Lipset, S. M., 1967, *The First New Nation* (Garden City, NY: Anchor/Doubleday).

Lipset, S. M., 1976, 'Radicalism in North America: A Comparative View of the Party Systems in Canada and the United States', *Transactions of the Royal Society of Canada*, series IV, vol. XIV, pp. 19–55.

Lloyd, P. C., 1971, *Classes, Crises and Coups* (London: MacGibbon & Kee).

Lukács, G., 1923 (1971), *History and Class Consciousness* (London: Merlin Press).

Lukes, S., 1973, *Émile Durkheim: His Life and Work* (London: Allen Lane).

Lukes, S., 1978, 'Power and Authority', in Bottomore and Nisbet, eds, pp. 633–76.

MacIver, R. M., 1926, *The Modern State* (London: Oxford University Press).

McKenzie, R. T., 1963, *British Political Parties* (2nd edn, London: Heinemann).

Maddison, A., 1982, *Phases of Capitalist Development* (Oxford: Oxford University Press).

Mallet, S., 1975, *The New Working Class* (Nottingham: Spokesman Books).

Mann, M., 1973, *Consciousness and Action Among the Western Working Class* (London: Macmillan Press).

Mann, M., 1986, *Sources of Social Power* (Cambridge: Cambridge University Press).

Mannheim, K., 1928 (1952), *Essays on the Sociology of Knowledge*, chap. 8, 'The problem of generations' (London: Routledge & Kegan Paul).

Mannheim, K., 1927 (1953), *Essays on Sociology and Social Psychology*, chap. 2, 'Conservative thought' (London: Routledge & Kegan Paul).

Marcuse, H., 1964, *One-Dimensional Man* (London: Routledge & Kegan Paul).

Marshall, T. H., 1950, *Citizenship and Social Class*, reprinted in Marshall and Bottomore, 1992.

Marshall, T. H. and Bottomore, T., 1992, *Citizenship and Social Class* (London: Pluto Press).

Marx, K., 1844, 'Contribution to a Critique of Hegel's Philosophy of Right'.

Marx, K., 1852, 'The Chartists', *New York Daily Tribune*, 25 August.

Marx, K., 1857–8 (1973), *Grundrisse* (Harmondsworth: Penguin Books).

Marx, K., 1859, *Contribution to the Critique of Political Economy*.

Marx, K., 1867, 1885, 1893–4, *Capital*, vols I, II and III.

Marx, K., 1871, *The Civil War in France*.

Marx, K., 1875, *Critique of the Gotha Programme*.

Marx, K. and Engels, F., 1845–6, *German Ideology*.

Marx, K. and Engels, F., 1848, *Communist Manifesto*.

Mayer, J. P. (ed), 1948, *The Recollections of Alexis de Tocqueville* (London: The Harvill Press).

Mead, M., 1970, *Culture and Commitment: A Study of the Generation Gap* (London: Bodley Head).

Meadows, D. H., Meadows, D. L., Randers, J. and Behrens, W. W., 1972, *The Limits to Growth* (New York: The New American Library).

Michels, R., 1911, (1966) *Political Parties* (New York: Free Press).

Middleton, J. and Tait, D. (eds), 1958, *Tribes Without Rulers* (London: Routledge & Kegan Paul).

Miliband, R., 1977, *Marxism and Politics* (Oxford: Oxford University Press).

Mommsen, W. J., 1974, *The Age of Bureaucracy* (Oxford: Blackwell).

Monnet, J., 1978, *Memoirs* (New York: Doubleday).

Moore, B., 1967, *Social Origins of Dictatorship and Democracy* (London: Allen Lane).

Morgan, L. H., 1877 (1974), *Ancient Society* (New York: Henry Holt).

Morris-Jones, W. H., 1971, *The Government and Politics of India* (3rd rev. edn, London: Hutchinson).

Mosca, G., 1896 (1939), *The Ruling Class* (New York: McGraw-Hill).

Myrdal, G., 1968, *Asian Drama* (New York: Pantheon).

Nadel, S. F., 1957, *The Theory of Social Structure* (London: Cohen & West).

Nettl, J. P., 1965, 'The German Social Democratic Party 1890–1914 as a Political Model', *Past and Present*, vol. 30, pp. 65–95.

Nettl, J. P., 1966, *Rosa Luxemburg* (London: Oxford University Press).

Nicolaus, M.,1972 ,'The Unknown Marx', in Blackburn, ed., pp. 306–33.

Nimni, E., 1991, *Marxism and Nationalism* (London: Pluto Press).

Nisbet, R., 1966, *The Sociological Tradition* (New York: Basic Books).

Nisbet, R., 1975, *Twilight of Authority* (New York: Oxford University Press).

Nisbet, R., 1978, 'Conservatism', in Bottomore and Nisbet, eds, pp. 80–117.

Oakeshott, M., 1952, *Rationalism in Politics and Other Essays* (London: Methuen).

Offe, C., 1972, 'Political Authority and Class Structures: An Analysis of Late Capitalist Societies', *International Journal of Sociology*, vol. II, no. 1, pp. 73–105.

Offe, C., 1976, *Industry and Inequality* (London: Edward Arnold).

O'Leary, B., 1989, *The Asiatic Mode of Production* (Oxford: Blackwell).

Oppenheimer, F., 1907 (1975), *The State* (New York: Free Life Editions).

Ortega y Gasset, J., 1930 (1961), *The Revolt of the Masses* (London: Allen & Unwin).

Ossowski, S., 1963, *Class Structure in the Social Consciousness* (London: Routledge & Kegan Paul).

Outhwaite, W., 1986, *Understanding Social Life* (2nd edn, Lewes: Jean Stroud).

Outhwaite, W., 1987, *New Philosophies of Social Science* (London: Macmillan).

Parekh, B. (ed.), 1975, *The Concept of Socialism* (London: Croom Helm).

Pareto, V., 1915–19 (1963), *Treatise on General Sociology* (New York: Dover Publications).

Parsons, T., 1969, *Politics and Social Structure* (New York: Free Press).

Peukert, D., 1991, *The Weimar Republic: The Crisis of Classical Modernity* (London: Allen Lane).

Pirenne, H., 1914, 'The Stages in the Social History of Capitalism', *American Historical Review*, vol. XIX, no. 3.

Piven, F. F. and Cloward, R. A., 1977, *Poor People's Movements* (New York: Pantheon Books).

Popper, K., 1945, *The Open Society and its Enemies* (London: Routledge & Kegan Paul).

Postan, M. M., 1967, *Economic History of Western Europe, 1945–64* (London: Methuen).

Poulantzas, N., 1968 (1973), *Political Power and Social Classes* (London: New Left Books).

Pribicevic, B., 1959, *The Shop Stewards' Movement and Workers' Control* (Oxford: Blackwell).

Renner, K., 1916, 'Problems of Marxism', part trans. in Bottomore and Goode, eds, 1978.

Renner, K., 1917, *Marxismus, Krieg und Internationale* (Stuttgart: J. H. W. Dietz).

Renner, K., 1921, 'Democracy and the Council System', in Bottomore and Goode, eds, 1978, pp. 187–201.

Richardson, L. F., 1960, *Arms and Insecurity* (Pittsburgh: Boxwood Press).

Rioux, M., 1965, 'Conscience nationale et conscience de classe au Québec', *Cahiers internationaux de sociologie*, vol. XXXVIII, pp. 99–108.

Robson, W. A., 1976, *Welfare State and Welfare Society* (London: Allen & Unwin).

Rokkan, S., 1961, 'Mass Suffrage, Secret Voting and Political Participation', *European Journal of Sociology*, vol. II, no. 1, pp. 132–52.

Ross, G., 1991, 'Eurocommunism', in Bottomore, ed., 1991.

Rudé, G., 1964, *The Crowd in History* (New York: John Wiley & Sons).

Runciman, W. G., 1969, *Social Science and Political Theory* (2nd edn, Cambridge: Cambridge University Press).

Sale, K., 1974, *SDS* (New York: Vintage Books).

Sartre, J-P., 1960 (1976), *Critique of Dialectical Reason* (London: New Left Books).

Schumpeter, J. A., 1919 (1951), 'The sociology of imperialisms', in *Imperialism and Social Classes*, edited with an introduction by Paul M. Sweezy (New York: Augustus M. Kelley).

Schumpeter, J. A., 1939, *Business Cycles: A Theoretical, Historical and Statistical Analysis of the Capitalist Process* (New York: McGraw-Hill).

Schumpeter, J. A., 1942 (1987), *Capitalism, Socialism and Democracy* (6th edn, London: Allen & Unwin).

Schumpeter, J. A., 1946 (1952), 'John Maynard Keynes', in *Ten Great Economists* (London: Allen & Unwin).

Scott, A., 1990, *Ideology and the New Social Movements* (London: Unwin Hyman).

Seton-Watson, H., 1964, *Nationalism and Communism* (London: Methuen).

Sivard, R. L., 1982, *World Military and Social Expenditures* (Leesburg, Virginia: World Priorities).

Skinner, B. F. 1971, *Beyond Freedom and Dignity* (New York: Alfred A. Knopf).

Skocpol, T., 1979, *States and Social Revolutions* (Cambridge: Cambridge University Press).

Smith, A. D., 1971, *Theories of Nationalism* (London: Duckworth).

Smith, R. C., 1978, 'The Changing Shape of Urban Black Politics: 1960–1970', *Annals of the American Academy of Political and Social Science*, vol. 439, pp. 16–28.

Sombart, W., 1906 (1976), *Why is there no Socialism in the United States?* (London: Macmillan Press).

Southall, A., 1968, 'Stateless Society', in *International Encyclopaedia of the Social Sciences*, vol. 15 (New York: Macmillan).

Stein, L. von, 1850 (1964), *The History of the Social Movement in France, 1789–1850* (Totowa, NJ: Bedminster Press).

Stojanović, S., 1973, *Between Ideals and Reality* (New York: Oxford University Press).

Tawney, R. H., 1921, *The Acquisitive Society* (London: Bell).

Tilly, C. (ed.), 1975, *The Formation of National States in Western Europe* (Princeton: Princeton University Press).

Titmuss, R. M., 1958, *Essays on the 'Welfare State'* (London: Allen & Unwin).

Tocqueville, A. de, 1835–40 (1946), *Democracy in America* (London: Oxford University Press).

Tocqueville, A. de, 1856 (1955), *The Old Regime and the French Revolution* (Garden City, NY: Doubleday).

Touraine, A., 1971a, *The Post-Industrial Society* (New York: Random House).

Touraine, A., 1971b, *The May Movement* (New York: Random House).

Touraine, A., 1973, *Vie et mort du Chili populaire* (Paris: Editions du Seuil).

Touraine, A., 1977, *The Self-Production of Society* (Chicago: University of Chicago Press).

Turner, B., 1978, *Marx and the End of Orientalism* (London: Allen & Unwin).

Turner, B., 1991, 'Asiatic society', in Bottomore, ed., 1991.

Turner, R. H. and Killian, L. M., 1972, *Collective Behaviour* (2nd edn, Englewood Cliffs, NJ: Prentice-Hall).

Wallerstein, I., 1974, *The Modern World System: Capitalist Agriculture and the Origins of the European World-Economy in the Sixteenth Century* (New York: Academic Press).

Weber, M., 1904–5 (1976), *The Protestant Ethic and the Spirit of Capitalism* (London: Allen & Unwin).

Weber, M., 1919 (1961), *Parliament and Government in a Reconstructed Germany* (English trans. as appendix to Weber 1921).

Weber, M., 1921 (1968), *Economy and Society* (New York: Bedminster Press).

Weber, M., 1923 (1961), *General Economic History* (New York: Collier Books).

Willener, A., 1970, *The Action-Image of Society* (London: Tavistock Publications).

Winslow, E. M., 1948, *The Pattern of Imperialism: A Study in the Theories of Power* (New York: Columbia University Press).

Wolf, E. R., 1970, *Peasant Wars of the Twentieth Century* (New York: Harper & Row).

World Bank, 1990, *World Development Report* (Oxford: Oxford University Press).

Wright, G. H. von, 1971, *Explanation and Understanding* (London: Routledge & Kegan Paul).

Wright, Q., 1965, *A Study of War* (2nd edn, Chicago: University of Chicago Press).

Zeitlin, I. M., 1971, *Liberty, Equality and Revolution in Alexis de Tocqueville* (Boston: Little, Brown & Co.).

Index

44   26

272752

This book is to be returned on or before
the last date stamped below.